BONFIRES OF THE AMERICAN DREAM IN AMERICAN RHETORIC, LITERATURE, AND FILM

BONFIRES OF THE AMERICAN DREAM IN AMERICAN RHETORIC, LITERATURE, AND FILM

DANIEL SHAVIRO

ANTHEM PRESS

Anthem Press
An imprint of Wimbledon Publishing Company
www.anthempress.com

This edition first published in UK and USA 2022
by ANTHEM PRESS
75–76 Blackfriars Road, London SE1 8HA, UK
or PO Box 9779, London SW19 7ZG, UK
and
244 Madison Ave #116, New York, NY 10016, USA

British Library Cataloguing-in-Publication Data
A catalogue record for this book is available from the British Library.

Library of Congress Cataloging-in-Publication Data
A catalog record for this book has been requested.

ISBN-13: 978-1-83998-382-5 (Hbk)
ISBN-10: 1-83998-382-5 (Hbk)

This title is also available as an e-book.

CONTENTS

CHAPTER 1

INTRODUCTION

Has there ever been a more (seemingly) heartwarming movie than Frank Capra's *It's a Wonderful Life*? Or one more steeped in anger, hatred, and resentment toward, not just the rich but also the poor and hapless, who hamstring and ruin George Bailey's life by triggering feelings of responsibility for their welfare? How reassuring is George's redemption, actually, when it requires the jokily depicted intervention of a dopey angel from Heaven? And why might the film have mutated, in viewers' eyes, from being "Communist propaganda" according to J. Edgar Hoover's FBI when it first came out (Johnston 2018, 3), to being the "perfect film for the Reagan era" (Wolcott 1986) just 40 years later?

Such questions help to show how works of popular art, and evolving audience reactions to them, can illuminate societal attitudes about status, class, and social mobility (among myriad other topics). *It's a Wonderful Life* is just one of the innumerable films, books, and other cultural products that can enrich our understanding of America's jumbled and ideologically freighted set of attitudes over time regarding the rich, the poor, and the "American Dream" of self-advancement and due reward.

Today, Americans are living through an era of unparalleled (since the Civil War) hatred and enmity between the members of different self-constituted groups, giving urgency to the question of how our social and political culture could have led us to so dark a place. Our long history of White supremacy, enforced both violently and through cultural norms, is obviously an important part of negative American exceptionalism. Yet, there is also our extraordinary lack of social solidarity, even just between Whites—manifested, for example, in widespread hostility, first to mask-wearing and then to vaccination, amid a pandemic.

An important element of this distemper involves the tension between egalitarianism and what I call market meritocracy. Egalitarianism of some kind, at least for White males, has been a core American value for centuries.

Exactly what it means, beyond its ruling out a titled nobility, is contested and unclear. The Declaration of Independence proclaims that all "men" (apart, perhaps, from Native Americans and enslaved persons[1]) are "created equal" and possess "certain unalienable rights," such as to "Life, Liberty and the pursuit of Happiness." These words appear to demand, at the least, some degree of equality in people's legal entitlements, and perhaps in how they are valued and respected. It can also readily be interpreted as demanding a degree of equality that extends to such real-world dimensions as the distribution of economic opportunity and political power. More controversially, it can be interpreted as condemning excessive inequality in people's economic outcomes, whether this involves poverty at the bottom or extreme wealth concentration at the top.

American egalitarianism's broader attitudinal fingerprints are apparent even when its meaning and demands are in dispute. I have elsewhere noted the long-standing American usage of "aristocrat" as a hostile epithet, rather than a term of self-description or respect (Shaviro 2020, 15). Likewise, to this day, "elite" and "elitism" are dirty words, which the members of particular elites not only disclaim as to themselves but also deploy disparagingly against the members of rival elites (115).

A second important strand of American ideology holds that, in a land that is ostensibly one of great opportunity, anyone can rise economically and socially—fulfilling the American Dream—through hard work backed by the requisite intelligence, self-discipline, and talent. Economic outcomes therefore rightly vary depending on each "man['s] [...] ability or achievement" (Adams 1931). This is a meritocratic view, under which market outcomes both depend on and reveal one's degree of personal worthiness. I call it *market* meritocracy because the worthy could instead be defined quite differently—based, for example, on test scores, religious faith, social skills, or athletic ability.

Market meritocracy ineluctably conflicts with egalitarianism if one views the latter as pertaining to ex post economic outcomes, not just ex ante opportunities. However, even insofar as the two are intellectually reconcilable, they are attitudinally in conflict in how they imply that one should view the rich and the poor. Under market meritocracy, both success and failure are truly and personally earned. Winners and losers are not equal after all—rather, the former are better and more deserving people than the latter. The rich owe the poor nothing—not even compassion or respect, and certainly not material aid through government.

---

1 The Declaration openly supports a Whites-only reading insofar as it refers to "merciless Indian savages" and complains that King George III has "excited domestic insurrections amongst us," referring to the threat of slave revolts.

Psychologically, no less than politically, this adds a nasty edge to the American Dream. Rather than just counseling supportively at the front end that one *can* succeed, it offers at the back end a potentially harsh judgment, depending on whether or not one *did*. Wealth becomes the supreme test, not just of how comfortably one will get to live but also of one's fundamental worth as a human being.

This not only raises the stakes regarding career outcomes but also promotes self-congratulation and lack of empathy. Moreover, it does so not just among the rich but also among those in lower economic strata who are eager to think of themselves as merely not rich *yet*. Consider Americans' frequently self-reported "unrealistic[] optimis[m] about their relative and absolute economic circumstances," such as a poll showing that "39% [...] believed that they either were already in the top 1% of wealth or 'soon' would be" (Graetz 2016, 807).

American Dream triumphalism, based on both real and imagined success, also helps to promote hatred and contempt for the poor. In this respect, it adds to the toxins already guaranteed by racism, given the widespread (and false) assumption among Whites that poor people are generally Black (see, e.g., Wetts and Willer 2018). Meanwhile, American Dream–fueled status anxieties may make it all the more urgent, for many Whites, to know of a subordinated group that will always, no matter what, rank below them.

While these dark byproducts of the American Dream can be seen across a wide historical spectrum, their virulence varies across time. The anxieties and hatreds grow stronger in eras, like our own currently ongoing Second Gilded Age, in which there is extreme wealth concentration at the top. Challenges to White supremacy may also feed anti-egalitarian and antidemocratic rage. Cultural works from different eras, and/or whose reception has differed as between eras, not only help to show this but can also aid one's struggle to understand it better.

In this book, I develop these themes by offering three in-depth case studies, each from a different expressive realm. The first is published rhetoric about success and economic merit. Here, I start with the "single most famous piece in all success literature" (Hilkey 1997, 92): Russell Conwell's *Acres of Diamonds* speech, which the author delivered more than 6,000 times between 1870 and 1925, thereby earning enough money to fund his establishing and endowing Temple University. I compare and contrast this speech with one that appeared in fiction several decades later: the 60-page, 33,000-word screed that the character John Galt purportedly delivers to the American public, on all radio channels, near the end of Ayn Rand's *Atlas Shrugged*.

As we will see, despite Rand's using a fictional character as her mouthpiece, the Galt speech consciously sets forth a "philosophy" that has found immense cultural resonance in America, extending to a wide swath of the economic and political elite (Duggan 2019, 78), as well as to millions who merely think about themselves optimistically. It overlaps ideologically with the *Acres of Diamonds* speech. Yet, rather than similarly using humor and conveying optimism, it is tellingly spittle-flecked with rage, grievance, and anxiety.

Second, from the realm of literary fiction, I examine F. Scott Fitzgerald's *The Great Gatsby*—a work that has come to be viewed as the "quintessential" (Cullen 2003, 180; Schudson 2004, 571) literary critique of the American Dream. *Gatsby* is perhaps a surprising choice for so culturally central a role, given its apparent view that inherited social rank is impervious to mere personally achieved wealth—in tension with the premises of both egalitarianism and market meritocracy. As we will see, however, its rollercoaster journey across time, from "flop" (according to Fitzgerald) when it first came out, to near-complete obscurity by the mid-1930s, to its post–World War II reemergence and canonization, and finally to its status today as required English class reading for millions of American middle and high schoolers, bears a relationship to broader economic and associated cultural changes.

Finally, from the realm of American popular filmmaking, I examine and compare Capra's *It's a Wonderful Life* and Martin Scorsese's *The Wolf of Wall Street*. These films prove to have a lot more in common than one might initially have thought. For example, each follows the career of an able young man who is born into the middle class, aspires ambitiously to achieve great things, chooses a career in finance, and runs there into legal peril that tests his loyalties.

The two films' commonalities help to sharpen their stark attitudinal and other differences. These reflect, among other things, the cultural gulf between the Americas of their respective eras. *It's a Wonderful Life*, although released in 1946, in many ways reflects attitudes from the Great Depression, during which much of it takes place. *The Wolf of Wall Street* mainly takes place in the late 1980s and 1990s, but it looks back at those years from a twenty-first century perspective that reflects multiple public subsequent exposures of business chicanery, ranging from the 2001 Enron scandal to the misbehaviors that helped trigger the 2007–2009 Great Recession. *Wolf* also seems strangely to anticipate the Trump era, reflecting the parallels between its featured grifter, Jordan Belfort, and the far more malignant one who would become the U.S. president several years later.

My primary focus will be on how these texts, and their changing reception across different eras, reflect core tensions in American culture, such as that between egalitarianism and market meritocracy. We may also, however, see occasional hints that the process of influence runs both ways. That is, popular works may themselves shape the broader culture in which they attract attention.

As case in point, Ayn Rand's shadow is large enough to raise the question of whether she has actually strengthened the political and cultural appeal of cruelty and selfishness, while also winning both mass and elite adherents to libertarianism (despite her stated distaste for it). Likewise, the genre of rogue-financier movies, dating back at the least to Oliver Stone's *Wall Street*, might reasonably be viewed as having shaped the malign aspirations, not just of the actual Jordan Belfort, but of countless others (e.g., Martin Shkreli).

The First Gilded Age ended peaceably, unless one attributes its full demise (after what historians call the Progressive Era) to the onset of World War I. Will the same happen to America's ongoing Second Gilded Age, and to the dystopian rage and discord that it has so energized? It is easier to hope so than to know. But if we do move on to brighter days, then perhaps tomorrow's books and films (if not long-form speeches, a dying cultural form) will help us better to understand the distinctive American cultural elements of the abatement.

CHAPTER 2

WINNERS AND LOSERS IN RUSSELL CONWELL'S *ACRES OF DIAMONDS* LECTURE AND THE JOHN GALT SPEECH IN AYN RAND'S *ATLAS SHRUGGED*

Introduction

Everyone is equal in America, but some are more equal than others. The American Dream is ostensibly available to all, even if recent social mobility data place us behind peer nations. However, suppose that, when (inevitably) some succeed while others fail, one believes both that the competition was fair and that the differential outcomes reflected disparities in merit, as distinct from either luck or morally arbitrary attributes that the market happens to reward. Then one may draw the conclusion that some people are fundamentally better than others, egalitarian platitudes to the contrary notwithstanding.

In eras of great economic inequality, those who sufficiently accept market meritocracy may therefore find it obvious, as did Theodore Dreiser (1931, 86), that "[t]he best that can be said for the [egalitarian] theories laid down in the Declaration [of Independence] is that they do more credit to the hearts of those that penned them than to their heads." If this view was sufficiently unchallenged, one might expect the rich to feel serene complacency regarding not just their entitlement to their wealth but also their proven superiority over the mass of people, entitling them to special respect and deference.

Yet egalitarian sentiments are not so easily dismissed. The less fortunate may view extreme material inequality as affronting egalitarianism, rather than refuting it. In an electoral republic, their views potentially matter, and at a minimum, their support (or, at least, passive acquiescence) must be courted. Even apart from this pragmatic issue, however, those at the top may have their own doubts about the fit between their status wishes and egalitarian values. This, in turn, may motivate them either to moderate, or to make all the more vehement, their claims to have been proven superior by economic success.

This chapter examines two prominent entries—from Russell Conwell and Ayn Rand—in the rhetorical literature that vehemently defends rich people's superior desert on market meritocratic grounds. In each, we can see the tension with egalitarianism, and the consequent importance of celebrating and even sacralizing economic success. However, in how they view ordinary people, as compared to members of the elite, Conwell and Rand are as different as sugar syrup and soured milk. This difference is of sociological, not just biographical, interest, given the contemporary following that each attracted.

Russell Conwell's *Acres of Diamonds* Speech

Let me say here clearly [...] ninety-eight out of one hundred of the rich men of America are honest. That is why they are rich. That is why they carry on great enterprises and find plenty of people to work with them. It is because they are honest men [...].

[T]he number of poor who are to be sympathized with is very small. To sympathize with a man whom God has punished for his sins, [and] thus to help him when God would still continue a just punishment, is to do wrong [...]. [L]et us remember that there is not a poor person in the United States who was not made poor by his own shortcomings, or by the shortcomings of someone else. (Russell Conwell, from the *Acres of Diamonds* speech [American Rhetoric version])

An instrument of social control?

Between 1870 and 1925, Russell Conwell gave the *Acres of Diamonds* speech to paying audiences thousands of times. It was heard or read by millions of people, and it made him millions of dollars. Given its mass outreach, its laudatory comments about the rich were not an instance of supper club-style self-congratulation among them. To representative audience members, the rich were people of great interest, but they were not "us."

The poor people whom Conwell disparages appear likewise not to have been mainly within the "us" category. Attendees generally had to pay a "liberal sum for a seat" (Shackleton 2008, 49). Moreover, while he invokes concern for poor people's welfare as a key reason for his speechmaking, he introduces the above-quoted dismissal of their deservingness in response to what sounds like an anticipated objection from compassionate, but nonpoor, audience members: "Some men say, 'Don't you sympathize with the poor people?' Of course, I do, or else I would not have been lecturing all these years.'"

The popular progressive historian Howard Zinn (2015, 262) views rhetoric such as Conwell's as a mechanism of social control. A "population dangerously concentrated in cities and factories, whose lives are filled with cause for rebellion, [must] be taught that all is right as it is [...] [and] that to be rich was a sign of superiority, to be poor a sign of personal failure." Yet, for such an account to be fully convincing, one must be able to explain it in terms of particular actors and their motivations. Thus, further questions of interest include the following:

- What was in it for Conwell? He was not being compensated by hidden puppet masters for preaching mass acceptance of inequality. He was catering to a commercial audience, and thereby earning money and fame, once he had stumbled, apparently fortuitously, into discovering the lecture's vast commercial potential (Shackleton 2008, 51).[1]
- Why would millions of people—not themselves rich, even if not mainly among the despised poor—have wanted to hear (and paid to hear) that rich people were better, not just better-off, than they were? Rather than being motivated to submit to social control as an end in itself, they presumably sought entertainment, encouragement, and advice. This may have related to Conwell's central claim that the "opportunity to get rich, to attain unto great wealth is [...] within the reach of almost every man and woman who hears me speak."
- Why is the *Acres of Diamonds* speech, in many respects, so distinctively odd? How does it invoke and appeal to egalitarian, as well as market meritocratic, sentiments—as it does—along the way to its teaching that the rich are better than the rest of us (at least, until we manage to join them), while the poor are worse?

---

1 Conwell called the *Acres of Diamonds* speech

  a mere accidental address, at first given [in 1869] before a reunion of my old comrades of the Forty-sixth Massachusetts Regiment, which served in the Civil War and in which I was captain. I had no thought of giving the address again [...] [until it] began to be called for by lecture committees.

An Acres of Diamonds *walkthrough*

The *Acres of Diamonds* lecture's central idea is that, in America, you can get rich right where you are.[2] "[I]n this country of ours every man has the opportunity to make more of himself [...] in his own environment, with his own skill, with his own energy, and with his own friends." It thus rebuts not just despair and defeatism but also the Horace Greeley adage, "Go West, young man."[3]

More generally, Conwell rambles comfortably over the following main themes:

1) *Stay where you are!:* The *Acres of Diamonds* lecture is named after its opening story, reportedly told to Conwell by an Arab guide while he was traveling in the late 1860s in what is now Iraq. The guide recounts the story of an ancient Persian named Ali Hafed, who had been a rich farmer in what is now India. Ali Hafed was happy until he heard about diamonds' immense value,

[...] whereupon he went to bed that night a poor man. He had not lost anything, but he was poor because he was discontented, and discontented because he feared he was poor. He said "I want a mine of diamonds," and he lay awake all night.

The next day, he sells his farm and embarks on a diamond-hunting quest across Asia and Europe. However, the quest fails, and "at last when his money was all spent and he was in rags, wretchedness, and poverty," he drowns himself in the Atlantic Ocean off Barcelona. But wouldn't you know it, with the sledgehammer irony of a *Twilight Zone* episode, it turns out that the farm he sold contained the now world-famous Golconda diamond mine.

Lest we dismiss this story as merely allegorical, Conwell then adds three modern versions that he insists are literally true. In the first, a California ranch owner unknowingly sells the site of the Sutter Gold Mine, in order

---

2 Conwell improvised the speech along a set pattern, rather than using exactly the same words each time. Moreover, it appears to have evolved over the decades, enabling him to stay current. This chapter amalgamates three versions that are currently available in writing. Each evidently dates from no earlier than the 1890s.

3 Greeley first said something like this as early as 1837 and was continuing to urge westward migration as the key to economic self-improvement as late as 1872. See Taylor (2015).

to gold-prospect fruitlessly in southern California. In the second, a Pennsylvania farmer who is eager to find oil becomes an expert in the business so he can work in it, sells his farm for $833, and rushes off to Canada. Alas, this causes him to miss out on the Titusville oil strike on his Pennsylvania land, which raised property values by hundreds of millions of dollars. In the last, a young man studies mining at Yale, while also working in the mining business for $15 a week. Offered a raise to $45 a week once he has graduated, this makes him so swellheaded that he declines it, sells his Massachusetts farm, and takes a mining job in Wisconsin. Here he earns just $15 a week in cash, but with what we would call an equity kicker in the event that he should discover valuable minerals. But, of course, he doesn't, and the site he sold turns out to contain a huge silver load. So "[t]hat professor of mines, mining, and mineralogy who knew so much about the subject that he would not work for $45 a week" misjudged land on which he had lived his whole life and benightedly "passed up a hundred thousand dollars [...] [that was] just for the taking."

These stories are perplexing. Is selling land inherently foolish on the ground that it always might turn out to hold fabulous hidden wealth? But then what about *buying* land, given the purchasers' windfalls? Is effort to improve one's prospects through diligent study or inquiry—pitilessly punished in each story[4]—a terrible mistake? Is the lesson to be learned that you *shouldn't* try to improve your chances, as great wealth will just come to you if you are patient and have faith? Yet how common are immense mineral strikes?

Rather than addressing any such questions, Conwell pivots to the takeaway, which is that metaphorical "acres of diamonds" are to be found everywhere, at least in the contemporary United States. For example,

[Y]ou have "acres of diamonds" in Philadelphia right where you now live [...]. Indeed, [t]here never was a place on earth more adapted [to the pursuit of wealth] than the city of Philadelphia today, and never in the history of the world did a poor man without capital have such an opportunity to get rich quickly and honestly as he has now in our city.

This brings him to the question of how, other than by fortuitously owning the Golconda or Sutter Gold Mines site, one can actually get rich while remaining in place.

---

4 Even Ali Hafed makes a stab at due diligence, by asking where diamonds are most likely to be found.

2) *Getting rich without a diamond mine:* Here again, Conwell instructs by (purportedly) real-world anecdote. He imagines a storekeeper from the back of the lecture hall asking why, if acres of diamonds are at hand, he has not grown rich by operating a corner grocery store for 20 years. Conwell explains, however, that this is the man's own fault. Suppose he had cared enough about his neighbors to get to know them intimately—where they were born, their family members, how they vote, and where they go to church. This would have enabled him to gauge their needs and stock the right items for them. Then "you would have been rich. But you go through the world saying, 'No opportunity to get rich,' and there is the fault right at your own door."

He offers numerous concrete examples purporting to show that, merely by observing what people want, one can get rich. A. T. Stewart had parlayed 62.5 cents of capital into a multimillion-dollar department store chain, simply by going door-to-door and asking people what they wanted to buy. John Jacob Astor had done the same in the fur business, by sitting on a park bench and discerning consumer taste from the bonnets that ladies were wearing. Numerous inventors, using common sense in lieu of technical expertise, had made huge fortunes by discerning public demand for such items as safety pins, rubber-tipped pencils, improved collar buttons, trout farms, and wooden toys.

Conwell asserts that no capital is needed for one to get rich overnight. Indeed, previewing an attack on male effeminacy that he develops further when denying that inherited wealth has any social significance, he mocks the "weak and dudish creature[s] […] [that] stand[] around the corners […] saying, 'Oh, if I had plenty of capital how rich I would get.'" To the contrary, a jackknife in a country store is capital enough. A. T. Stewart's 62-1/2 cents had been enough.[5]

The fact that customers benefit from having their wants satisfied provides a rationale for allowing profit. A just price is neither too high nor too low. Had Conwell, in his days as a teenage clerk in his family's country store, responded to repeated requests for jackknives by stocking them,

---

5 Its being, apparently, so easy to get rich once one opens one's eyes and starts paying attention raises the question of why pulling up one's current stakes, like Ali Hafed did, should be so affirmatively harmful. The answer might be that it is unnecessary, distracting, and requires one to learn from scratch about a whole new set of people and local conditions.

I would have actually done [the customers] a kindness, and I would have received a reward myself, which it would have been my duty to take [...]. I have no more right to sell goods without making a profit on them than I have to overcharge [...] dishonestly beyond what they are worth.

This raises, however, the broader question of how capitalist free enterprise can be reconciled with Christian piety.

3) *Reconciling profit and Christianity:* Conwell spends a great deal of time reconciling the profit motive with piety. Getting rich is indeed a Christian duty, despite the "awful mistake of these pious people to think you must be awfully poor in order to be pious." They fail to see that "[M]oney is power, and [that] you ought to be reasonably ambitious to have it [...]. [Y]ou can do more good with it than you could without it. Money printed your Bible, money builds your churches, money sends your missionaries, and money pays your preachers." Secular uses are fine as well, however. For example, "they that own their own homes are made more honorable and honest and pure, true and economical and careful, by owning the home."

What about the Bible's statement that money is the root of all evil? Conwell notes, however, that the full quotation holds that the *love* of money is the root of all evil. This, he explains, is merely the problem that we today might call fetishizing money for its own sake. One should honor money's uses, not the thing itself. So the Bible, ostensibly, was merely condemning "the miser that hoards his money in the cellar [...] [rather than] invest[ing] it where it will do the world good." It was not disparaging the determined and even paramount pursuit of material self-interest.

Conwell's defense of the profit motive has a dual character. He is legitimizing profit both as a proper aim for everyone in his audience and as something that the A. T. Stewarts and Astors are wholly entitled to keep (or at least spend). Indeed, they are entitled, not just to use their wealth but also to be admired and emulated for having gained it. This brings us to his celebration of rich people—pampered heirs aside—as paragons who, despite (or perhaps because of) their demonstrated superiority, turn out also to honor fully the spirit of American egalitarianism.

4) *Celebrating rich people:* Conwell asserts that 98 out of 100 rich people are honest, and that this is why they are rich. However, while to be rich is to be honest, it does not equally follow that to be honest is to be rich. One must also be kind, observant, thoughtful, attentive to others' wants, and unswayed by the fallacy that worldly materialism is irreligious.

Rich, self-made Americans, we learn, almost invariably have the egalitarian virtue of being "simple, plain, everyday people" who live modestly. Like Abraham Lincoln, they do not "strut[] around altogether too large to notice an ordinary working mechanic," in the manner of a "puffed-up balloon." Lincoln notwithstanding, however, only businessmen, not political leaders or army generals, are systematically to be admired. Businessmen "do[] great deeds with little means and [...] accomplish[] great purposes from the private ranks of life." Political office, by contrast, can never make one great, even if some great men have held office. This follows logically from the fact that, in a democracy, "the people rule [...]. [Hence,] the office-holder is but the servant of the people, and the Bible says the servant cannot be greater than the master."

When honest businessmen like John D. Rockefeller and Andrew Carnegie find themselves hated, this is only because the newspapers have been lying about them. A rich friend of Conwell's—from the context, perhaps Rockefeller—has asked him privately why so many should deem him "the blackest-hearted villain that has ever trod the soil," when in fact (as Conwell avers) "he is one of the sweetest Christian men I ever knew." The answer, apparently, is envy. Anyone who earns 100 million dollars will be lied about, and "you can judge your success in any line by the lies that are told about you."

Much of the blame for this mudslinging belongs to labor unions, along with radical orators who condemn the "oppressive rich" and tell "honest working men" the "lie" that they are "nothing but slaves." Any true patriot will instead "endeavor with all his soul to bring the capitalists and the laboring man together until they stand side by side, and arm in arm, and work for the common good of humanity. He is an enemy to his country who sets capital against labor or labor against capital."

5) *Inherited wealth:* Inheritance poses a challenge to Conwell's schema. People who inherit great wealth have neither personally earned it nor needed to deploy the character traits that he associates with becoming rich. In addition, insofar as they use their parents' resources to make money for themselves, this might be viewed as competitively unfair, and in tension with the claim that all Americans have an equal opportunity to succeed.

Conwell's response to these challenges is startlingly aggressive. Heirs, he suggests, are generally contemptible and worthless people. But not to worry, they are so certain to founder on their supposed advantages—which are actually grave disadvantages—that dynastic wealth transmission is not, even in the slightest degree, a real-world issue in America.

If young men who whine that they need capital are pathetically effeminate, in Conwell's viewpoint, they have nothing on those who actually inherit capital. These mincing, lisping, foppishly dressed "specimen[s]" draw such descriptions from him as "human crickets," "grasshoppers," "gobbler turkeys," and "poor, miserable, contemptible American monkeys." They dress in fancy clothes that prevent them even from sitting down, they cannot drive their own fancy cars, and they are physically too weak even to "carry paper and envelopes twenty feet."

This reflects their upbringing, and specifically their (otherwise so admirable) parents' mistakes. If only rich parents would make their sons work for everything, the latter would

get the discipline of a poor boy that is worth more than a university education to any man [...]. [But] as a rule, the rich man will not allow his son to work – and his mother! Why, she would think it was a social disgrace if her poor, weak, little lily-fingered, sissy sort of a boy had to earn his living with honest toil.

One can readily imagine plebeian audiences' delight at these broad strokes, which use homophobic stereotypes to mock the seemingly fortunate. Conwell's sallies also, however, help to rebut any critique of dynastic wealth transmission as in tension with market meritocracy. Rather than just denying that one needs capital, such as from one's parents, in order to get rich, he positively asserts that being born rich is an immense disadvantage. "It is no help to a young man or woman to inherit money [...]. It will curse you through your years [...]. I pity the rich man's son." Indeed, he asserts that statistics from Massachusetts show that "not one rich man's son out of seventeen ever dies rich." While "[t]hey are raised in luxury, they die in poverty." So America, within the lifespan of a single generation, is the land both of rags to riches and of riches to rags.

6) *The poor:* Conwell's attitudes regarding poor people are more complex than what he has to say about the rich. Given all the opportunities that they must have squandered, they are not to be sympathized with and are merely suffering God's just punishment. Yet he "would not have been lecturing [all] these years" if he did not feel sympathy for the poor. What resolves any contradiction is the fact that today's poor, if only they would take his advice, could easily become tomorrow's rich. Poverty reflects bad

attitudes, but these can be fixed at any time. In a market economy, no less than in church, there is always still hope of salvation for everyone, and the spirit of Christian charity demands addressing the sinners most of all.[6]

Reconciling egalitarianism with market meritocracy

The *Acres of Diamonds* speech spans the period from the very start of what we now call the Gilded Age to the mid-1920s. Later versions acknowledge the growing sociological divide between labor and capital, and the "discouraging gloom" that has grown as workers, however mistakenly, "begin[] to feel [...] held down" by the "aristocratic money-owner" whom they believe does not care about them.

Yet the speech's spirit embodies the manic excitement about getting rich that was prominent in popular culture in the early 1870s, and that, as I have noted elsewhere, preceded the actual Gilded Age takeoff in high-end inequality (Shaviro 2020, 136). Thus, a tool that may have proved useful for social control emerged before this very use might have started diminishing its credibility.

Conwell could scarcely be more vehement than he is with regard to markets as an almost perfect tool for administering distributive justice. However mindlessly random one may find the outcomes in the speech's introductory stories about diamond and gold mines, its main body insists that both rich and poor invariably get what they deserve—as a matter not just of economic productivity, but also of honesty, insight, and concern about others. He dismisses muckraking exposés of the rich as merely the work of lying, envious journalists along with unpatriotic outside agitators.

Within the upper classes, Conwell favors the business elite over any rivals that it might have. Hence, his dismissal of political leaders as mere public servants, and his mocking a learned professor of mineralogy as such a blind, conceited dunce that he failed to see, "right next to the gate" on his family homestead, "a block of native silver eight inches square."

Such crowd-pleasing flourishes, topped by his mockery of the effete young fops who have been cursed with family riches, imply a socially egalitarian impulse that is borne out in other ways as well. Again, the rich must be "simple, plain, everyday people" to merit full praise. Their talents lie in empathy and observation, not in towering genius or a mastery of esoteric skills. They are closely connected to the mass of consumers who (to mutual benefit) make them rich.

---

6 It should come as no surprise that this sounds like evangelical Christianity. Conwell became a Baptist minister in 1880, or 10 years after, he had started giving *Acres of Diamonds* lectures.

Moreover, members of the audience must be flattered, no less than amused. Their reason for paying "liberal sum[s]" to hear a paean to the rich is that the speech is also, and indeed primarily, a self-help guide. It would presumably have been hard for Conwell to sell out lecture halls, telling people that their failures to date are not only their own fault, but irredeemable. He further courts a popular audience by mixing stories about his close friends among the rich and famous with mockery of his foolish younger self, as in the tale of the jackknives that he failed to stock.

Conwell's vision of marrying egalitarianism to market meritocracy might have worked all the better, and proven more enduring, had it been more true. Suppose it were actually the case that only 1 out of 17 fortunes lasts beyond a single generation and thus that the social classes are continually being reshuffled like a poker deck. This might lead to paralyzing anxiety—or, perhaps, fierce efforts by the rich to rig the game on behalf of their children—but at least it would not have yielded alienating social stratification.

Conwell also offers something of a small-town vision, despite its claimed applicability to the likes of Philadelphia. Many of his stories involve a local producer, gauging and satisfying his neighbors' tastes. This helps to make it somewhat dated even as an account of the First Gilded Age's economic transformations, which relied crucially on an increasingly integrated national marketplace. Its datedness may initially have added to its charm, but also guaranteed that its manner of negotiating the tensions between egalitarianism and market meritocracy would eventually need to be reformulated.

The John Galt Speech in Ayn Rand's *Atlas Shrugged*

[You have] reach[ed] the stage of self-abasement where you seek to make the concept "human" mean the weakling, the fool, the rotter, the liar, the failure, the coward, the fraud, and to exile from the human race the hero, the thinker, the producer, the inventor, the strong, the purposeful, the pure. (From John Galt's speech in Ayn Rand's *Atlas Shrugged*)

The Randian vision

Self-confident people generally find it easier to stay calm than do the insecure and self-doubting, who may be prone to rage spasms and to hurling insults. Likewise, self-confident people generally need not lavish outsized praise on themselves, while the insecure may need to wallow in grandiose self-celebration, marinated in self-pity and feelings of victimization. Donald Trump is a prominent recent example.

With that in mind, consider how Ayn Rand, through her mouthpiece John Galt, depicts the world's supposed two types of people during his 33,000-word, 60-page radio speech at the climax of her novel *Atlas Shrugged*. At its beginning, we are told of Galt's extraordinarily calm and reflective tone. He "sound[ed] as if he were speaking here, in this room, not to a group, but to one man; it was not the tone of addressing a meeting, but the tone of addressing a mind." But then we get to read the speech itself.

When Galt discusses the bad type of person (i.e., not his own), he calls them—in a single breath!—all of the following: (1) weaklings, (2) fools, (3) rotters, (4) liars, (5) failures, (6) cowards, and (7) frauds. Over the full course of the speech, he stretches out considerably more, also variously deploying the terms (8) mindless brutes, (9) looting thugs, (10) mooching mystics, (11) grotesque little mystics, (12) parasites, (13) cannibals, (14) irrational, (15) dishonest, (16) unjust, (17) incompetent, (18) mediocre, (19) zeroes, (20) thieving loafers, (21) sniveling neurotics, (22) self-loathing neurotics, (23) castrating eunuchs, (24) savages, (25) pigmies, (26) criminals, (27) knaves, (28) grotesque little atavists, (29) prostitute[s], (30) stupid, (31) impotent, (32) frantic, and (33) scum.

Given the speech's ostensible two-hour length, Galt manages to offer up a fresh insult more than once every four minutes. His insult usage rate more than doubles, however, if one considers repetition. For example, "parasite" and "savage" come up 12 times each and "cannibal" 7 times. There are five repetitions of "thug" and four of "brute." If this is the "tone of addressing a mind," it must be that of a tantrumming eight-year-old boy.

At the same time, Galt complains that people of the bad type are consumed by fear and hatred. Moreover, they disrespectfully "fail[] to give recognition to man's mind" – that is, to people of his type, they being the only ones who actually have minds.

What about people of his own type? Galt explains that they are heroes, thinkers, producers, inventors, strong, purposeful, and pure. They are men[7] of justice, independence, reason, wealth, productive genius, and, perhaps best of all, self-esteem. That is, each has "inviolate certainty that his mind is competent

---

7 Despite Rand's gender, the Galt speech scarcely mentions women. In this section, I will follow her terminology of referring continually to "men," because that most accurately represents the mindset on display.

to think, and his person is worthy of happiness." Thus equipped, they single-handedly, through the pure power of deep, abstract, solitary thought, create skyscrapers, electronic tubes, supersonic airplanes, atom-smashing engines, and interstellar telescopes, without which the savages would still be living in hovels. Yet the savages grant them less dignity than cattle—figuratively whipping and enslaving them, riding on and eating them.

Galt's savages and heroes are largely synonymous with the masses and the rich, respectively. While one's type is not fixed by one's parents' classification, bequests do little to complicate the picture. We learn elsewhere in *Atlas Shrugged* that the man who is "fit to inherit wealth" does not need it, as he would "make his own fortune no matter where he started." Meanwhile, if an heir is not "equal to his money […] it destroys him."

What could inspire such anger against the masses and grandiosity concerning the rich? One can almost see spittle dampening the pages. As a matter of biography, Rand experienced the distressing convulsions of the Russian Revolution and the initial Stalin years. Born in Saint Petersburg, Russia, in 1905, she came to America in 1926, and the "structure of feeling that runs throughout [her] work was forged in counter-revolutionary Russia" (Duggan 2019, 32).

Moreover, as a matter of personal psychology, she appears (at least, in the Galt speech) to present a textbook case of narcissistic personality disorder. The most recent Diagnostic and Statistical Manual of Mental Disorders (DSM-5) defines this condition as involving a pervasive "pattern of grandiosity, need for admiration, and lack of empathy." Those suffering from it are "preoccupied with fantasies of unlimited success, power, […] [or] brilliance," believe that they are too "special or unique" to be understood by anyone less extraordinary, and "display snobbish, disdainful, or patronizing attitudes." Yet their "[v]ulnerability in self-esteem makes […] [them] very sensitive to 'injury' from criticism […], which may leave them feeling humiliated, degraded, hollow, and empty," causing them to "react with disdain, rage, or defiant counter-attack." This is essentially the Galt speech in a nutshell.

Yet the popularity of Rand's work requires a broader sociological explanation, not just one pertaining to her as a distinctive individual. After all, her U.S. fan base is huge, and her cultural impact here is "incalculable […]. [Her] influence is ascendant across broad swaths of our dominant political culture—including among public figures who see her as a key to the zeitgeist, without having read a word of her writing" (xiii–xiv). Thus, notwithstanding her work's alien origin and distinctive psychological roots, but as proven by its mass appeal, it expresses a widely felt American response to issues of class and distributive desert.

Rand published her most influential works, the novels *The Fountainhead* (1943) and *Atlas Shrugged* (1957), amid the mid-century Great Easing. Thus, both were written at a time of reduced high-end inequality, relative both to 50 years before and 50 years later. But while each of these two works immediately attracted a large following, only in the last few decades have they reached their full cultural ascent. So their evidently broad appeal says as much about our era as about either her original milieu or America when she was writing them.

Rand fans come in two main demographic groups, with overlapping membership at different life cycle stages. First, as young adult fiction, her work speaks to innumerable adolescents (mainly boys) who are going through "the usual 'the world is persecuting me and doesn't see my true genius' phase that momentarily afflicts the typical high schooler," reflecting an age-appropriate predilection for "immature self-pity" (Sirota 2013). Second, among adults, Rand has a mass following that extends below the top 1 per cent, including, for example, rank-and-file conservative activists (Gibson 2011). However, she appears to have special appeal within a sector of the economic and political elite that comprises the likes of "wealthy bankers, CEOs, tech moguls, and right-wing politicians" (Duggan 2019, 78). These people are successful enough that one might have thought they would be less inclined than Randite teenagers to embrace a narrative so drenched in vitriol and self-pity.

The sociological roots of Rand's appeal to her elite followers are well captured by a fan letter regarding *Atlas Shrugged* that the famous Austrian economist Ludwig von Mises sent her in 1958. Von Mises congratulates Rand for her attacks on the "academic prattle" of "self-styled 'intellectuals.'" In addition, he thanks her for "hav[ing] the courage to tell the masses what no politician told them: you are inferior and all the improvements in your conditions which you simply take for granted you owe to the effort of men who are better than you" (von Mises 1958).

Von Mises was an intellectual outlier at the time, and one thus can understand his resenting fellow intellectuals who were proponents of the then-dominant centrist liberal mainstream economic and political consensus. Yet it is initially harder to understand why he, and many American-born Randites as well, both then and now, would take such solace from Rand's having the "courage to tell the masses [...] you are inferior." As we will see, however, the impulse furiously to resent people who are less fortunate than oneself persists in American culture, reflecting the tensions around (and between) egalitarianism and market meritocracy.

The context and main arguments of the Galt speech

While *Atlas Shrugged* is fiction, it is sufficiently didactic in both tone and content to contain lessons for the reader that are no less express and specific than those in Conwell's *Acres of Diamonds* lecture. This is especially true of Galt's radio speech, which Rand spent two years writing and considered the best short expression of her philosophy. This speech's context and central argument can be summarized as follows.

Atlas Shrugged is set in a dystopian future that nonetheless has elements in common with contemporary (1950s) America, for which it is an intensified allegorical stand-in. Indeed, all that makes it worse than the present is the continued ramping up of welfare state policies and politics that it suggests would be intolerable, as a matter of principle, whether vast or mild in scope.

The book's original working title was *The Strike*. Rand changed this, however, to avoid giving away the central plot twist, which is the rise of a Galt-led movement by "men of reason" to withdraw completely from society, ending their productive contributions to it, and thereby setting it up for rapid collapse. They do this in response to the intolerable violation and insult of their being taxed, regulated and otherwise harried within the mixed economy of a modern welfare state.

Given that tax obligations, like other legal obligations, can be enforced at gunpoint if necessary, imposing them involves impermissible violence against the producers. Galt's core syllogism in this regard has been paraphrased as follows: "Taxes are illicit use of force; self-defense when confronted with illicit use of force is moral; therefore our program of economic and maritime terrorism that will kill millions of people is moral as it is self-defense" (Bradley 2016).

Galt views any mandatory transfer from the creators to the parasites as economically destructive. It induces the "man of productive genius [to] bec[o]me a destroyer of wealth, choosing to annihilate his fortune rather than surrender it to guns." More importantly, however, from a moral as opposed to practical standpoint, requiring such transfers is the "essence of evil." Proponents of the welfare state are not merely "misguided idealists [...] [but] anti-living objects who seek, by devouring the world, to fill the *selfless* zero of their soul [*sic*]. It is not your wealth that they're after. Theirs is a conspiracy against the mind, which means: against life and man."

Galt's "proof" is metaphysical. For any living organism, its life is its fundamental value. Men are thinking beings, who use their reason to live, and whose purpose is to serve their own lives and happiness. Thus, because "existence exists" and "A is A," rationality necessarily equates to people doing only as they wish, in exclusive pursuit of their own happiness. "A" would have to be "not A" for a starving man to have any right to compel the transfer of a penny (such as through taxation) from a rich man. When the poor (or the state on their behalf) compels the redistribution of a penny, the rich man does not merely become a penny poorer by reason of the transfer, but is being vilely subordinated. His very mind and existence are being negated and denied. He is being treated like a prey animal or a slave, in violation of the fundamental axiom that "existence exists."

In the face of such provocation, and of the moral crisis brought on by the doctrine of sacrifice that purports to justify it, Galt has chosen to "destroy[]" your world" through the producers' strike. No relevant moral considerations weigh against thus triggering mass destruction. Rationality commands only that "no man [...] *initiate*—do you hear me? no man may *start*—the use of physical force against others." Once the cannibals have started the violence, such as by imposing even minimal tax obligations via the state, this insult, and its horrific, irrational assault on the human mind (i.e., on the producers, who are the only ones with minds), would suffice to justify a violent response.

There is a difference between the speech's broadly stated policy conclusions, on the one hand, and its emotional and dignitary aspects, on the other hand. Rand, through Galt, is not the only one ever to argue for a libertarian social vision, based on entitlement to the fruits of one's own labor, and reasoning from there to inviolable property rights and the illegitimacy of all government redistributive policy, including that of even a minimal welfare state. But dividing the world into heroes and cannibals, and viewing the latter as viciously oppressing the former, so that the rich are despised and exploited slaves of the poor, is a more distinctive contribution. So is the sense of existential insult and threat that fuels the speech's evident emotional attraction to the notion of violence and mass destruction as an act of revenge.

Galt / Rand versus Conwell

While Ayn Rand and Russell Conwell are obviously very different figures, they bear comparison. Although they wrote decades apart, each uses market meritocracy to make the case for rich people's deserving their wealth and poor people their hardships. Each emphasizes not just the practical reasons for accepting unequal market outcomes but rich people's moral superiority over poor people.

They employ, of course, very different styles. Conwell relies mainly on anecdotes; Galt on purported axioms. The fact that Galt, unlike Conwell, is not actually a live person, speaking to a live audience, helps to explain his being so uningratiating and humorless. These differences do not, however, explain his being so much angrier than Conwell.

Galt's venomous denunciations of people outside his own group do not, of course, prevent him from insisting repeatedly on his own pure "rationality," in contrast to the "irrationality" of the "savages," whom he views as stewing and steeping in their "reservoir of hatred." We are left to our own inferences regarding why, amid America's relatively placid 1950s, Rand should find the wealthy's circumstances so intolerably hurtful that the book's dystopian future should be deemed to offer an instructive and revelatory parable concerning the present.

In the *Acres of Diamonds* lecture, Conwell complains about the "prejudice against rich men because of the lies that are told about them." Yet, despite the social unrest and labor strife of the late Gilded Age and the Progressive Era—far greater than that of the 1950s—this is merely an annoyance, not a sign of the apocalypse. "Give me your check for one hundred millions," Conwell recounts telling the rich friend who may be Rockefeller, and "I will take all the lies along with it." In this and other instances, Conwell offers for our view a person of greater mental health than Galt (for all Galt's sputtering about "neurotics"), blessed with both a more secure ego and a better grasp of reasonable proportionality.

However, the differences between the *Acres of Diamonds* lecture and the Galt speech go well beyond their setting their emotional balance dials at 5 and 11, respectively. They also treat common topics very differently. Consider their contrasting views of the following:

Inventors: Conwell's inventors are plain folk at heart who use common sense and an understanding of what people need to invent the likes of safety pins and rubber-tipped pencils. Galt's inventor, far more grandiosely, is "a man who asks 'Why' of the universe, and lets nothing stand between the answer and his mind."

Apportioning credit between the brain and the hands: Conwell notes that people call General Grant

the man who put down the rebellion [...]. [But d]o you think we would have gained a victory if we depended on General Grant alone? [...]. [His tomb on the Hudson River] is there because he [...] represented two hundred thousand men who went down to death for this nation and many of them as great as General Grant.

Now consider Galt on skyscrapers. If thousands worked on the construction site, and many died in industrial accidents, this would earn them no share of the credit for the end result. They would still just be "[d]rifters and physical laborers [who] live and plan by the range of a day." All honor would go to the great visionary who created the skyscraper in his mind.

Who can succeed?: Conwell sounds, for a moment, almost like Galt when he says that, if another man "has one hundred millions, and you have fifty cents, [...] [then] both of you have just what you are worth." Both agree that the poor are wholly to blame for their own failures. Yet Conwell views no one as irredeemable. Anyone can still get rich through effort plus an attitude adjustment.

To Galt, by contrast, the rich and the poor verge on being members of different species. They bring to mind the contrast, in H. G. Wells' *The Time Machine*, between the Eloi who live peacefully on the earth's surface and the vile Morlocks who prey on them from below ground. To be sure, the Eloi—meek and feeble-minded creatures whose ancestors' intellectual refinement has devolved into mere pleasure-seeking—are nightmare photo negatives of Galt's sturdy champions, rather than being their peers. The Morlocks, however, could scarcely be more like the masses in Galt's speech, other than in their having become cannibals and parasites literally, rather than just figuratively.

Given the gross inferiority of Galt's thugs and savages, none of them could ever create anything of value. They completely lack the needed mental equipment. Being incapable of thought and reason, they can only prosper by stealing the creators' wealth.

Is the speech directed to Everyman?: The *Acres of Diamonds* lecture clearly is addressed to Everyman, even if the typical audience member was well-off enough to pay a "liberal sum for a seat." Moreover, while it disparages the poor as Others whom God has cursed, it also offers them hope, albeit at the price of social and political quiescence. It treats the entire society as engaged in a conversation in which the poor are participating and worth addressing.

The Galt speech, by contrast, is not for the self-styled Everyman, even though Rand presumably sought (and indeed got) mass sales for *Atlas Shrugged*. Within the novel's plot, Galt ostensibly is speaking to the entire nation, via the radio channels that he has commandeered for the speech. This includes all the brutes and thugs, sometimes addressed in the speech as "you," whom he is evidently eager to insult and threaten.

But consider the speech's actual prospective readers. If you self-identify as a person of justice, reason, and self-esteem, then Galt is wheedling and flattering you, through your presumed inclusion in so superior a breed. But if you think of yourself as just a regular, ordinary person, he is insulting you. For readers to identify with a speech that, in von Mises' description of the novel, says "you are inferior and [...] owe [everything] to [...] men who are better than you," they almost have to be assuming that "you" is other people, not themselves. This may be a clever sales strategy—implicitly flattering millions of readers with the presumption that they, unlike their peers, are exceptional. Yet it treats poor people, and ordinary ones more generally, as outside the conversation. They are too stupid and irrational to be worth addressing, other than in the language of insult and threat.

With respect to the masses, the Galt speech offers more than a whiff of eliminationism. While he does not openly advocate mass murder, his so vehemently denying their basic humanity pushes clearly in that direction. They ostensibly lack minds, any capacity for thought, and any shred of decency, dignity, or ability. They are parasites, cannibals, savages, and thugs, accused of violence against the "Men of Justice," whose right of violent self-defense he trumpets. Under Galt's view, it seems clear that just killing them all, if feasible, would be both a needed and a justified safety measure, to be implemented without the slightest hesitation, pity, or regret.

Intellectuals: Professional intellectuals, such as academics, do not fare well in either text. Conwell, however, settles for gently mocking the professor who vainly overrates his labor value and misses the giant silver lode under his feet. Galt, by contrast, vomits his hatred of "intellectual hoodlums" such as the "seedy little smiling professor who assures you that your brain has no capacity to think," and who "takes pleasure in crippling the mind [sic] of his students."

Economic class and exploitation: Both Conwell and Galt deny that the rich are exploiters, guilty of expropriating the fruit of poor people's labor. Both agree that the rich, rather, are great public benefactors who better other people's lives, no less than their own. Only Galt, however, living in the era of the modern welfare state, reverses the critique and insists that the poor are savagely exploiting and expropriating rightful gains from the rich.

Why so harsh?

As the above comparisons help to show, while both the *Acres of Diamonds* lecture and the Galt speech defend the superiority and entitlement of the rich, their stances in doing so differ sharply. Conwell tries, to a degree, to reconcile egalitarianism and market meritocracy. His way of doing so may lose persuasiveness insofar as inherited and other sources of capital make more of a difference than he concedes, and if opportunity is therefore unevenly distributed. Still, his poor and rich are linked by the former's reasonable aspiration to join the latter, and by the latter's retaining a homespun democratic style.

Reconciling egalitarianism and market meritocracy could not possibly be further from Rand's agenda. Rather, she aims to bury egalitarianism and stomp on its grave. To her, the masses and the rich are so unequal and different that any sense of connection between them is impossible. There also appears to be no middle ground between pure exemplars of the two types. So far as the distribution of intellect or character is concerned, Galt appears unfamiliar with the concept of a Bell curve. Rather, some people are geniuses, while most are morons.

Within this oddly bimodal distribution of intellectual ability and morality, the great appear to be especially narrowly clustered. Moreover, not only are they always wholly good (albeit, in some cases, too willing to accommodate the scum), but they invariably get along with each other perfectly. They recognize each other on sight, never have conflicting interests, and interact purely through voluntary trade that is unruffled even by disputes regarding who should get more of the surplus that they realize by transacting to mutual advantage.

Those who belong to the masses, by contrast, are unfailingly stupid, untalented, and contemptible. They have no dignity and serve no broader social purpose (reflecting that there is no such thing). Given, moreover, that altruism is a dirty word in Rand's lexicon, a man of genius can reasonably leave any of them to die, without feeling regret, if their inevitably feeble and pathetic efforts to sustain themselves should fall short.

Even as sharply hierarchical visions go, this is an uncommonly vicious one. Consider, by contrast, the classic European aristocratic social conception of centuries past, under which, as I have noted elsewhere, "the great and humble owe each other a kind of mutual respect, involving the exchange of gracious patronage for grateful deference" (Shaviro 2020, 12). In Galt's vision, the great have vastly benefited the poor, but only as an incidental byproduct of efforts that they undertook purely to satisfy themselves. Awe and deference are rightly owed upward, but only as the tributes inherently due to mind and reason. And nothing but indifference and contempt will ever travel back downward.

Why should so curdled and angry a social vision have appealed, over the years, to so many millions of Americans? Comparisons are in order, both to an idealized version of aristocratic hierarchy and to Conwell's far more benign version of market meritocracy.

Randian versus aristocratic hierarchy

Suppose that, in a given society, everyone has an accepted station that is known from birth. Who you "are" is just a question of your ancestry. This might have been the case under a pure, idealized version of western Europe's aristocratic societies some centuries back. While one doubts that this vision ever came close to being fully realized, its even partial truth may have sufficed for it to influence social attitudes and perceptions.

Such a vision stands far from satisfying modern social ideals, under which we value people's having the opportunity to improve their social (as well as economic) standing, based on who they are as individuals, and what they do. Yet, unappealing though it may be on balance, it has at least the virtue, by reason of its predetermined certainty, of tamping down status conflicts. People who know and accept where they stand in the hierarchy, and who view this as reflecting the natural order of things, may then at least be less driven by anxiety and disappointment to look for enemies.

Now consider a competitive market society in which people do not know in advance whether they will succeed or fail. Suppose, moreover, that they are competing, not just for more money versus less, but also for the pride and honor that attach to success, versus the shame and disgrace that attach to failure. In a country like the modern United States, the relevant battles start early. Even children (backed by anxious parents) compete over test scores, school admission, and grades, long before they are old enough for the battles to move to the workplace.

As Daniel Markovits (2019, x) has written, the resulting meritocratic competition "entices an anxious and inauthentic elite into a pitiless, lifelong contest to secure income and status through its own excessive industry." Meanwhile, such competition "drives the middle class to resent the establishment [...] [and] ensnares the society that both classes must share in a maelstrom of recrimination, disrespect, and dysfunction." Whether one has unmistakably joined the elite or merely aspires to do so, Randite anger, grandiosity, and self-pity offer a way of responding psychologically to such pressures.

The fact that we also still have egalitarian ideals may further heighten the acrimony. Egalitarianism offers a pushback tool for the less successful against the more so, especially if the former can challenge the contest's fairness. America's vast and increasingly transparent inequality of opportunity assures that these grievances will be both prominent and credible. Meanwhile, so long as we retain democratic political institutions, the winners have reason to worry about their grip on all the gains that they have reaped. Political leaders, chosen by a mass electorate, have extensive powers to challenge the rich via taxation, regulation, and law enforcement.

Among the superrich, fear of the mass electorate triggers "a mix of aggressiveness and perceived embattlement." Accustomed to extreme deference in their daily lives, they find it humiliating and intolerable when they must "run to the political class hat in hand" (Marshall 2014). What is more, such feelings can radiate down the social scale, to middle class and working people who identify with the superrich and/or hold similar fears regarding their own market rewards.

In common parlance, we call people "middle class" even if they are well above the 90th percentile (Noah 2012, 145). This reflects that you truly are in the middle, at least within your own mind, if you see people both above and below yourself, and—whatever the two groups' actual relative numbers— you assign them comparable social weight. Choosing to identify with either group—the rich or the poor, as compared to oneself—may lead to one's viewing the other group as the enemy.

People who are in the middle, in this sense, but who choose to identify with the top may therefore readily embrace a John Galt view of poor people as lazy, threatening, parasitic, and exploitative—not to mention, as being far luckier than they themselves are, by reason of a supposed exemption from facing any need to struggle or work. The *Wall Street Journal* (2002) epitomized such a view when it labeled as "lucky duckies" the people who are too poor to owe current year federal income taxes.

Why is Rand so much harsher than Conwell?

The above discussion suggests that, in the contemporary United States, anxieties within the creed of market meritocracy, helped along by the creed's tension with egalitarianism and democratic institutions, can help to explain the venom and fury of so widely embraced a social artifact as the Galt speech. These forces do not, of course, make the adoption of such attitudes inevitable, at least for a given individual. People can react to the stresses in many different ways, including with benignity and tolerance rather than hatred.

Against this background, Conwell and Rand are just two individuals who happened to have attracted large followings at different times. Moreover, each one's approach may have had proponents at both times. Nonetheless, it is worth asking why the rancor of a John Galt should have such widespread cultural and political resonance today.

One important change since Conwell's time has been the rise of mass media and digital culture. People are effectively more isolated today, in self-chosen virtual and infotainment bubbles. These are ready instruments for glamorizing success, promoting "good versus evil" narratives, and demonizing those who differ from the members of the target audience. Randism is well adapted to flourish in such an environment.

By contrast, the *Acres of Diamonds* lecture shows the hallmarks of its having been honed and repeatedly delivered in an era characterized by small-town culture and shared public spaces. Even Conwell's Philadelphia appears to be a place where the rich and the poor know each other as neighbors. Personal familiarity can breed tolerance that loses oxygen in a far-flung and disparate mass society.

Conwell also relies on the apparent credibility of his claim that anyone can get rich, simply by paying close attention to his advice. Hope is an important mood sweetener in his relatively benign and optimistic version of market meritocracy. People today, however, may suffer emotionally from being less credulous. U.S. data suggest that upward mobility has declined in recent decades. Americans have increasingly both done worse than their parents and reasonably come to fear that their children will do worse than they themselves have. Thus, anxiety may now sour the atmosphere as much as credible happy talk once sweetened it.

A further leading suspect on the modern American crime scene is the rising perceived threat to White supremacy. The civil rights movement was already triggering White anxiety when *Atlas Shrugged* first appeared in 1957. Yet in that era Blacks still ranked far below Whites, both socially and economically. They were demanding equality, but it was far from clear that they could soon get it (or that they would be anything but grateful if they did).

In recent years, millions of White Americans have evidently felt deeply wounded and aggrieved by such developments as the two-term presidency of a dignified Black man, the demographic threat that Whites will soon become a numerical minority, and the effrontery (from their perspective) of protests against police murder and monuments honoring Confederate traitors. Today's Trumpist, Fox News-led fury over such faux outrages as a given Black athlete's refusal to salute the American flag, or the supposed reign in the public schools of "critical race theory," reflect a fearful sense that White supremacy not only is collapsing, but might even soon be reversed.

Racism is not just about animus, but about the need to feel that one is better than other people. Personal failure and disappointment are easier to tolerate if one can at least feel securely superior to a group of despised Others. Moreover, such palliatives are all the more necessary if one's ideology celebrates economic winners while heaping scorn on the losers. Thus, America's twin ideological toxins—newly endangered racism and pitiless market triumphalism—have recently been working in concert to trigger anxious Galtian rage.

Galt, Rand, and ressentiment

In the end, Galt's 60 pages filled with insults, anger, and grandiosity bring to mind a strangely top-down or backward version of the mental state that Friedrich Nietzsche famously dubbed "ressentiment." Under a standard definition (from Wikia), ressentiment involves one's feeling a

> profound sense of resentment, frustration, and hostility directed at that which one identifies as the cause of one's frustration, generated by a sense of weakness/inferiority and feelings of jealousy/envy […] [This] ultimately generates a […] value system or morality that exists as a means of attacking […] the perceived source of one's own sense of inferiority.

Its essence is scapegoating and blame deflection, and one adopts it to help one cope with self-loathing.

Nietszche viewed ressentiment as expressing "slave morality" in response to the masters' greater strength and self-confidence. For Rand followers, however, the mechanism may be different. Already anxious about their own status and worth, and feeling further threatened by egalitarian values and democratic institutions, along with challenges to White supremacy, they externalize the threat to a hate object that seemingly lies below them, rather than above. The poor, they decide, are the enemy—sponging off them, dominating and humiliating them, getting away with irresponsible behavior, and perhaps even laughing at them. Rand, through Galt, unwittingly puts on display the slave morality of the weeping, impotent would-be and should-be master, who imagines that his withdrawal from a society that fails to appreciate him will trigger its swift collapse and the plebeians' humble pleas for his triumphant return as their acknowledged master.

Consider how obsessed Galt seems to be with dominance and subordination. Even a minimal, tax-funded social safety net means that "any man who fails is your master; if you fail, any man who succeeds is your serf." It means that "*[y]ou* are the only servant, the rest are the masters, *you* are the only giver, the rest are the takers, *you* are the eternal debtor, the rest are the creditors never to be paid off." It means you face the "whip" and are "enslaved." The wealthy are victims, forced to do penance for their virtues, commanded to "surrender" and "submit." Even just "the subordination of your mind to the mind of another;

the acceptance of an authority over your brain" is "the vilest form of self-abasement and self-destruction."

Piling up the insults as usual—just one or two, it seems, is never enough—Galt complains that modern welfare states sacrifice the "rational" man to the "irrational, the independent man to parasites, the honest man to the dishonest, the man of justice to the unjust, the productive man to thieving loafers, the man of integrity to compromising knaves, the man of self-esteem to sniveling neurotics." This is a nightmare of existential subordination, no matter how small the actual burden might be, or how great the market rewards that one still gets to retain. Even if it is just a penny, "we are [being] chained and commanded to produce by savages," who are eager to "deny and destroy [our] mind[s]." This a "rational" man simply cannot bear.

Making this all the worse, Galt craves others' genuflection, rather than just that he be spared it himself. "[W]e have lived among you, but you failed to know us, you refused to think and to see what we were." The cannibals have "failed to give recognition to man's mind." They should have honored the great and acknowledged their own worthlessness, rather than inverting the proper social order.

In sum, the John Galt we see in the speech feels threatened, wounded, and humiliated by modern political and fiscal institutions. He responds by lashing out venomously against the would-be masters. To this end, he promulgates a value system centered on attacking those enemies as contemptible and vile. He wraps around himself, so vehemently as to suggest pathetic neediness, the mantle of genius, virtue, reason, and the exclusive possession of "mind." He thereby deflects the blame for his inability to fulfill his own sorry fantasies of omnipotence.

Randism and Trumpism

A final salient point about Randism is its clear association, whether as cause or related cultural product, with the political rise of Trumpism. As Lisa Duggan (2019, 89) notes,

> Trump is in most ways a Rand villain—a businessman who relies on cronyism and manipulation of government, who advocates interference in so-called 'free markets,' who bullies big companies, who doesn't read. His personal and public corruption mirror her character sketches of sellouts and dirtbags.

He also invokes nationalism and aligns with fundamentalist Christianity, both of which she reviled. Yet Trump not only praises Rand and led an administration filled with her acolytes, but truly embodies her spirit, in particular via his attachment to cruelty and derision. By celebrating "winners" while heaping hatred and scorn on "losers," he gained a devoted following drawn from both the very successful and the more rank-and-file.

Racism feeds Rand's popularity, as it does to Trump's, given that her "impassioned defense of hierarchy [is] embedded in the history of racial capitalism and imperialism, combined with a eugenic sense of the greater value of [White] physical beauty and capacity" (Duggan 2019, 53). However, each is also a proponent of hating other Whites, be they Rand's "cannibals" or many of the targets of Trump's unceasing rants. Racism therefore need not be always overtly at center stage. With or without it, however, those who embrace Rand's (and Trump's) overheated fantasy identification with exalted "winners," accompanied by hatred of degraded "losers," as a way of salving their own frustrations and self-doubt, invite the very mockery that they fear.

Summary: Negotiating the Tension between Twinned Values

Both egalitarianism and market meritocracy are deeply embedded in American ideology and culture. Indeed, even the famous statement in the Declaration of Independence that "all men are created equal" goes on to offer fodder for market meritocracy, not just for egalitarianism. It states that all men "are endowed by their Creator with certain unalienable Rights, [and] that among these are Life, Liberty and the pursuit of Happiness." An equal right to *pursue* happiness is quite distinct, of course, from any equal right to achieve it or to enjoy equal access to its material prerequisites.

The mention of liberty, no less than that of the pursuit of happiness, can be deployed in favor of immunizing market outcomes from egalitarian challenge. Moreover, while the Declaration of Independence has nothing to say about the supposed moral superiority of those who succeed over those who fail, the very fact that we are otherwise all deemed equal may serve, in practice, to motivate wanting to make such claims. Both the lack of other grounds for special distinction (such as noble birth) and the threat of egalitarian pushback by the poor against the rich may create a taste for being acknowledged as fundamentally better—not just as more fortunate.

The twinning of egalitarianism with market meritocracy creates problems for anyone who wants to push toward either favoring or disfavoring the rich. For each side, one of the two values helps, but the other presents obstacles. Spokespersons on the right, such as Conwell and Galt/Rand, must somehow denature egalitarian critiques of wealth inequality. Those on the left face instead the challenge of explaining why principles of liberty, and of privileging only the *pursuit* of happiness, do not support exempting unequal market outcomes from criticism.

In both the *Acres of Diamonds* lecture and the Galt speech, we see evidence of how difficult this challenge can be on the right—which is not to say that it is easier on the left. In each of these two works, the strain of countering or neutralizing egalitarianism shows up in startling ways.

Conwell's clearest tells come whenever he goes beyond mere boosterism to leave basic credulity far behind. In particular, this happens when he argues, not just that one can overcome a lack of access to capital, but that it has no bearing on economic success. He reaches even greater absurdity by claiming that inheriting a large fortune leads almost inexorably (16 times out of 17!) to personal economic ruin. While he is echoing the Andrew Carnegie type of fear, widespread in American culture at the time, that those who are born to luxury will be spoiled and weakened by it, he takes things improbably far, for what appear to be ideological reasons. Conwell's views of inheritance and capital permit him to deny that there is any such thing as inequality of opportunity—unless, perhaps, it favors the poor over the rich. By thus protesting too much, he inadvertently underlines the force of the critique that he needs to sideline.

Galt's fury over the insult apparently posed to "men of reason" by egalitarianism and democracy is even more startling. One struggles to see why, in a country so generally prosperous and mainly peaceful as America has long been, the whiff of eliminationism that he offers should have been so enthusiastically inhaled by so many, over so many decades.

In this regard, it surely matters that mass murder (at least of Whites) has not within memory been a project potentially in view in America. Denying millions of people's basic human qualities so thoroughly that they might seem unworthy to live is arguably a different sort of exercise in a mainly peaceful country than in one where genocide might actually be within view. Against a sufficiently peaceful background, even such viciously dehumanizing denigration as Galt's may be, in the main, a fantasy exercise, meant no more seriously than killing video game characters. Still, it bespeaks a hysteria that reeks of unease deriving from a pathetic need to be accepted as a great winner, and as vastly superior to the average person. And even mere fantasy violence can lead over time to the real thing.

CHAPTER 3

PESSIMISM FOR OPTIMISTS AND VOYEURISM FOR PESSIMISTS IN F. SCOTT FITZGERALD'S *THE GREAT GATSBY*

Contours of the American Dream

The only thing worse than success is failure. Achieving your goals can prompt restiveness once the sugar rush has faded. Is that all there is? Was it worth the price? Did you deserve it? But if you failed, was it your fault? Are you a loser? Were you cheated? Unlucky? If you failed, does that mean that you have nothing? Or indeed that you *are* nothing?

What we call the "American dream of a better, richer, and happier life for all our citizens of every rank" (Adams 1931, xx) invites asking oneself such questions. By counseling the pursuit of success, at the risk of finding failure, the American Dream valorizes personal aspiration and effort, in lieu of seeking contentment where one is. Yet, even if this has benign societal effects, the battle for success can prove unsettling for both winners and losers, prompting them to focus on whether the effort was worth it and on whether the game was fair or fixed. The American Dream thereby helps to give a sociologically distinctive color to Americans' anxieties about social rank, personal satisfaction, and personal desert.

Although the American Dream is an "omnipresen[t]" cultural concept— to many, "the most lofty as well as the most immediate component of [...] American identity" (Cullen 2003, 5)—it has no single fixed meaning. Most obviously, it focuses on upward economic mobility. Yet, it also connotes the pursuit of ends as specific as home ownership and as vague or general as personal fulfillment.

Likewise, rather than being a "dream of merely material plenty" (Adams 1931, 405), or of "motor cars and high wages merely [...] it is a dream of [people's] being able to […] attain to the fullest stature of which they are innately capable […] [so that they will] be recognized by others for what they are" (404). By succeeding, you gain not just material goods but due respect from other people. If you *do* better than the average person, that implies that you *are* better.

For the American Dream to be fully realized, people's opportunities to "attain to the fullest stature of which they are innately capable […] [must be] regardless of the fortuitous consequences of birth or position" (404). This is a vision of purely individualistic striving within a featureless social landscape. Believers in the American Dream assert that the requisite consignment of birth and position to their rightful irrelevance "has been realized more fully in actual life here than anywhere else, though very imperfectly even among ourselves" (405).

The American Dream's breadth and indeterminacy invite using literary fiction to help us in apprehending it. In this regard, one particular novel stands out as an obvious choice. By nearly—though not quite—universal consent, F. Scott Fitzgerald's *The Great Gatsby* is the "quintessential" (Cullen 2003, 180; Schudson 2004, 571) literary exposition or critique of the American Dream.[1] It holds this place even though the term "American Dream" was not invented until 1931, when the popular historian James Truslow Adams made it the centerpiece of his bestselling book, *The Epic of America*, whereas *The Great Gatsby* was published in 1925. Historians largely agree, however, that Adams was describing (even if also adapting) a long historical tradition, with roots going back to the New England Puritans, the Founding Fathers, and the Horatio Alger/Russell Conwell era, as well as being embodied in millions of American immigrants' expectations when they came to America (see, e.g., Cullen 2003, 5).

To some readers, *Gatsby* is "simultaneously enchanted and repelled" by the American Dream (Fussell 1952, 293) or finds it "irresistible," although a "mirage" (Corrigan 2014a, 9). To others, *Gatsby*'s pessimism goes further, exposing the Dream as "little more than a thinly veiled nightmare […] [awash in] waste, desolation, and futility […] that resound with the chords of moral horror and disillusion" (Bicknell 1954, 556–57). Yet if this harsh reading were clearly right—and even more so if the exact terms of its purported excoriation of American ideals were clearer—*Gatsby*'s canonical mainstream cultural standing would be quite perplexing. It is, after all, the book most universally assigned to

---

1 For a dissenting view regarding *Gatsby* and the American Dream, see Decker (1994, 67–68).

American middle- and high-school students. Exposing the American Dream as a hideous sham is not, presumably, a central pedagogical goal of middle- and high-school curriculum boards.

Supporting the boards' complaisance, probably few of *Gatsby*'s captive student readers find it so wholly denunciatory. Indeed, to some, it is "just a boring [love story] about rich people" (Corrigan 2014a, 3). Others, with greater pleasure and surprise, may find a lurid, voyeuristic drop-in to a world of decadent glamor, like that which Baz Luhrmann offered in his 2013 film version of *Gatsby*. Still, others may find that it connects powerfully, at an emotional level, with their own still vague and ambivalent hopes and fears regarding what adulthood may look like for them.

These differing impressions reflect *Gatsby*'s deliberate ambiguity regarding whether, at its core, it is about the quest for success, or the world of rich people. Fitzgerald could easily have written and organized it in such a way as to make it clearly one of these two things, far more than the other. Instead, he chose to give competing prominence to each.

Suppose *Gatsby* had simply followed the title character's life story in chronological order. We thus would first see his poor childhood and wandering teen years, followed by his sudden reinvention when the rich yachtsman Dan Cody takes him on board, followed in turn by his military induction, affair with Daisy, wartime experiences, postwar destitution until he meets his second sponsor (the gangster Meyer Wolfsheim), and thenceforth straight through to the end. This would unmistakably be an American Dream story above all— Horatio Alger with an arsenic twist.

Now suppose instead that the book had followed the same time sequence that it actually does, but with a just-the-facts narrator, less poetry and symbolism, and no Jay Gatsby backstory beyond the fact of his recent crime-fueled rise from poverty. Then the book's predominant focus on the customs of the super-wealthy, including the apparently circumscribed social prospects of the merely nouveau riche, would likewise be clear. Instead, however, *Gatsby* leaves room for both perspectives regarding its primary focus.

Gatsby's Journey from Flop to Cultural Icon

These days, at least in the United States, *Gatsby* is easily the most widely read work of American literature. It has been called "America's greatest social novel about class" (Corrigan 2014a, 14). More particularly, the topics of broad sociological interest that it addresses include upward mobility, the born rich versus the nouveau riche, and how class relates to race.

All this plus *Gatsby*'s relationship to the American Dream make it a natural (or even inevitable) target of inquiry for a study such as this one. Yet the grounds for taking an interest in it pertain not just to the text itself but also to the history of its cultural reception. Somewhat of a flop when it first came out in 1925, *Gatsby* had virtually disappeared from view by the time of Fitzgerald's death in 1940. By 1945, however, it had entered a period of startlingly brisk and steep rediscovery by the public, and reassessment by literary critics, who now often focused on its relationship to the American Dream. By 1960, *The New York Times* could deem it "safe now to say that [*Gatsby*] is a classic of twentieth-century fiction" (Lucey 2013).

More recently, while *Gatsby* has remained as culturally prominent as ever, its high-end scholarly eminence has faded somewhat since its 1950s critical heyday (Corrigan 2014a, 272–74). As early as the mid-1960s, some began to disparage it as middlebrow (see, e.g., Scrimgeour 1966). Meanwhile, its place in popular culture has been altered both by its having become so iconic and by the onset of America's Second Gilded Age.

Gatsby's cultural import has therefore evolved through four distinct periods. The first three were those of its appearance, disappearance, and revival. The fourth I will call its post-iconification period. We will see that, when optimism about upward mobility was high, *Gatsby* was rapturously viewed (at least by literary critics) as offering a harsh evaluation of the American Dream—making it, in effect, pessimism for optimists. By contrast, in the present era—generally a less hopeful one regarding Americans' individual prospects for upward mobility—it is more a vehicle for exciting escapism, inviting a glamorous wallow in the world of great privilege that it depicts. It thereby now functions, at least for popular audiences, more as voyeurism for pessimists.

Reading a (Somewhat Didactic) Work of Literary Fiction

This chapter's switch in genre from the didactic lectures discussed in Chapter 2 to a work of literary fiction such as *Gatsby* has methodological implications. Both Conwell in the Acres of Diamond lecture and Rand in the Galt speech could scarcely have aimed more at giving their audiences clear and specific messages. By contrast, Fitzgerald in *The Great Gatsby* is consciously aiming to create a work of art within a well-developed literary tradition that values ambiguity, open-endedness, and deliberate under-specification (show, don't tell).

Yet, for this particular work of fiction, the distance from the didactic lectures is less than it would have been if one were reading, say, the work of a Lewis Carroll or a Samuel Beckett. *The Great Gatsby* uses realist conventions to examine a particular time and place. Moreover, it reflects a degree of deliberate didactic intent, focused in large part on sociological commentary. Fitzgerald called himself a "moralist at heart" and said that he wanted to "preach at people" (Schulz 2013, 4).

Gatsby is most clearly didactic when it addresses the topic that Fitzgerald "preached about most […] the degeneracy of the wealthy" (4). As we will see, it illustrates, with little ambiguity, his beliefs about how and why, as stated in his nearly contemporaneous short story, *The Rich Boy*, "the very rich […] are different from you and me." There, thus, is little room for flexible interpretation of his portrait of Tom Buchanan, the book's preeminent representative of America's most privileged, or even of Tom's wife (Gatsby's inamorata) Daisy.

Then there are the specific moral and/or aesthetic judgments that *Gatsby*'s first-person narrator, Nick Carraway, offers regarding its title character and what happens to him. Gatsby had at first "represented everything for which I have an unaffected scorn." Yet there proved to be "something gorgeous about him," and he "turned out all right at the end." Gatsby's "belie[f] in the […] orgastic future that year by year recedes before us […] [as] we beat on, boats against the current, borne back ceaselessly into the past," makes him no less heroic than doomed.

These are not just idiosyncratic judgments about a particular fictional character. Their broader sociological content is made clear by *Gatsby*'s treating its characters—most of all, but not just, its mythified title character— as "ideographs" (Trilling 1945) or social archetypes who are deliberately rendered flatly (Rothman 2013).

Yet the book's judgments about Gatsby and what happens to him are harder to pin down than its very clear viewpoint about the Buchanans. Not only are the verdicts that Nick shares with us themselves ambiguous, but he may not be a reliable narrator. Consequently, other than in its view of the rich, *Gatsby* offers readers "a Rorschach test. Some see it as a celebration of the decadence of wealth, and others see it as a fable warning of the repercussions of that shallow lifestyle" (Chalupa 2013). Likewise, some, following Nick's lead, find Gatsby's fervid embrace of hollow illusions to be gloriously ennobling. Others view the lesson learned as precautionary, in the sense of its demonstrating the deadliness of a self-deluding obsession with the past.

Such ambiguities make reading *The Great Gatsby* very different from reading the Acres of Diamonds lecture or the Galt speech. They prove, moreover, to be crucial to the book's capacity to speak in different ways to people in different eras. In particular, they help to support its dual character as a pessimistic text for optimists and a voyeuristically escapist one for pessimists.

The Great Gatsby in the 1920s

The Gilded Age versus the Jazz Age

Fitzgerald first thought of the story for *The Great Gatsby* while in Long Island in the spring of 1924 (Flanagan 2000)—perhaps not far from the spot where its title character stares across the bay at the Buchanans' mansion. The book's thorough immersion in the "irresponsible world of American wealth in the early twenties" (Berryman 1946) adds to its capacity to provide contemporary social commentary. Yet Fitzgerald initially planned to set the story in 1885 or right in the middle of the Gilded Age (Canterbery 1999, 297).

This may have reflected a view that the 1920s were sufficiently like the Gilded Age—widely viewed, with good reason, as a plutocratic era in which the wealthy towered high above the rest—for the earlier era to serve as a stand-in for the later one. And indeed, Tom and Daisy Buchanan's arrogance and sense of entitlement bring to mind characters who were born to wealth in literature that is set in the Gilded Age. Consider George Amberson Minafer in Booth Tarkington's *The Magnificent Ambersons*. George's distasteful arrogance, rooted in an extreme sense of inherited superiority that is wholly undimmed by his family's having been rich for just two generations (since 1873), allows readers to enjoy, if also to pity, his wholly deserved and complete "comeuppance" (as the novel calls it).

Moreover, while Jay Gatsby, as a bootlegger, could not, as such, have been a Gilded Age figure, works from that era likewise feature insecure arrivistes whose arrival at high wealth levels collides with their lack of the requisite breeding and social self-confidence. Consider William Dean Howell's *The Rise of Silas Lapham*. Here the eponymous lead character, having earned a sudden fortune through the paint business, finds himself so lost amid, and overwhelmed by, Boston high society that he actually is relieved when he loses his fortune and must return to his prior home in the rural outlands.

Despite such parallels, which help to make sense of Fitzgerald's initial impetus to set the story in the 1880s, he gained a great deal by choosing instead a contemporary Jazz Age setting. Most obviously, this enabled him to supply the glittering backdrop that eventually proved so crucial to the book's mass appeal. In addition, it allowed him to present the social tensions around wealth as not just the product of huge inherited fortunes. *Gatsby* goes well beyond being a "return to normalcy" story (in Warren Harding's famous phrase), in which peacetime and the end of the Progressive Era allow for the resumption of Gilded Age social practices. It shows as well how recent social changes have altered the dynamics around wealth inequality.

One important change that *The Great Gatsby* depicts extensively—in tension with its central thesis about the dominance of inherited wealth—is the rise, not just of new fortunes like Gatsby's but of a new and very modern type of alternative social elite. Consider the "zany collection of nouveau riche immigrants as well as theater and movie people" (Corrigan 2014a, 97) who flock to Gatsby's parties. Gatsby says that he likes to keep his house "full of interesting people [...] who do interesting things. Celebrated people." They include, for example, a "moving-picture director and his Star" who are so famous that even Tom and Daisy gawk at them. Tom disparages the party guests by saying "I don't know a soul here." Yet, "stung to envy by Gatsby's wealth and glamorous guests" (Fitter 1998, 9), he cares enough about the figure he cuts there to complain when Gatsby keeps introducing him to strangers as "the polo player."

All this helps to show that relationships at the top are not quite as simply vertical as in, say, the New York of Edith Wharton's *The House of Mirth*—set just 20 years earlier. Wharton shows her heroine Lily Bart, in the course of her decline, passing through one distinct social set after another, each with its own leaders, main places, and practices. In Wharton's New York, however, these circles' relative ranks are absolutely clear, and those in the lower ranks generally would welcome promotion (or even just being noticed by those from above). It is not so clear that Gatsby's nouveau riche businesspeople and celebrity artistes would generally be thrilled by the chance to gain entrance to Tom Buchanan's world. Indeed, for those from Tom's tier who are more self-confidently venturesome and less over-the-hill than he is (we are told that he peaked at age 21 and has faced "anticlimax" ever since), it might even be the other way around.

A second important feature of *Gatsby*'s social world involves the 1920s rise of White racial anxiety. In 1924, while Fitzgerald was writing *Gatsby*, the Ku Klux Klan achieved a new historical membership peak (Michaels 1995, 23). The Klan's revival had less to do with any fresh challenges to the subordination of African Americans than with several years of roiling controversy over immigration, in particular by non-"Nordic" immigrants from Europe (Decker 1994, 59–60). Anti-Semitism was especially prominent in the mix, at a time when neither Jews nor others from eastern and southern Europe were coded socially in America as White to the degree that they are today.

White hysteria responded, not just to immigration itself but also to the rise of organized crime. Prohibition, by creating bootlegging, had "propelled organized gangsterism to new heights" and induced a broader "association of immigrants with lawlessness" (60). *Gatsby* openly adverts to this with its stock anti-Semitic portrayal of Wolfsheim, whom Fitzgerald makes sure we will understand is based on Arnold Rothstein (by then infamous for having reportedly conspired to fix the 1919 World Series).

A third important change that we can see in *Gatsby* was the rise of mass consumer culture and a new "ideology of consumption," shaped by advertising that could trigger "intensive consumer tantalization" centered around ever-changing fashions (Fitter 1998, 7). *Gatsby* extensively depicts the importance both of fetishized high-end consumer objects and advertising. Thus, consider Daisy's "orgasmic" (Posnock 1984, 208) response to Gatsby's piles of beautiful new shirts—she actually weeps as she fondles them. Or consider her telling him that he always looks so "cool […]." "[y]ou know [, like] the advertisement of the man," when she is at last expressing her love for him in front of Tom. The relationship between this aspect of the 1920s culture and *Gatsby*'s fascination with free-floating aspiration and desire would reemerge as a topic of scholarly interest in the post-iconification period.

Gatsby's view of the rich

On the subject of the superrich, even if Fitzgerald is not quite a reverse Conwell or Galt—condemning arrogance, rather than exalting greatness—still, he chooses to be very straightforward and clear. According to *The Rich Boy*, what makes the "very rich […] different from you and me" is that "[t]hey possess and enjoy early, and it does something to them, makes them soft where we are hard, and cynical where we are trustful […]. They think, deep in their hearts, that they are better than we are." In *Gatsby*, this early-imbibed self-confidence—and its lack among those not born rich—helps Tom Buchanan rapidly to crush Gatsby, whose assumed persona "br[eaks] up like glass against Tom's hard malice" once he is exposed as a cheap crook—shamed more by the cheapness than the crookedness—and as "Mr. Nobody from Nowhere."

Then there is Nick's famous judgment near the end of *Gatsby*: "They were careless people, Tom and Daisy—they smashed up things and creatures and then retreated back into their money or their vast carelessness, or whatever it was that kept them together, and let other people clean up the mess they had made." This comes after Daisy has killed Myrtle Wilson while driving Gatsby's car, but declined to step forward and take responsibility, while Tom has deliberately brought about Gatsby's death by siccing the grieving George Wilson on him. So the smashing with which they are charged here is not just metaphorical.[2]

---

2 Jordan Baker, who is in the Buchanans' social circle but not as wealthy, calls herself "careless," for not realizing that Nick, like her, is a "bad driver" rather than an "honest, straightforward person." Here, however, not only is the resulting smash-up that she experiences just metaphorical, but she, not others, is the one who bears its ill consequences. The Buchanans only hurt others through their carelessness.

The book's moral condemnation of the Buchanans is enhanced by their relatively monochromatic presentation. The other main characters can be viewed from multiple angles. Gatsby, for example, is both a flashy tough and a misty-eyed dreamer. Jordan Baker is languid and dishonest (according to Nick), but also capable of being moved by Gatsby's story about Daisy, and of having her feelings hurt when Nick "thr[ows her] over on the telephone." Nick is a self-styled moralist who boasts early on about his extraordinary honesty, but Jordan finds him to be otherwise. His passivity and withdrawal add mystery to his self-portraiture.

Tom Buchanan, by contrast, could scarcely be less ambiguous. The novel's words and phrases, when discussing him, fall into a narrow range. They include, for example, hard, supercilious, arrogant, dominance, aggressively, cruel, fractiousness, paternal contempt, stronger, more of a man, and restlessly. Tom looks the same from all angles, and no sympathetic reader of the novel could view him favorably.

Daisy is a bit more ambiguous. From the outside, we get a lot of the male gaze, albeit focused more on her social type than her physical attributes. From the inside, we see her sadness and ambivalence about the path with Tom that she chooses both on their wedding day and again at the novel's climax. We also get to see—as she does—that Gatsby's demands of her are unaccompanied by any interest either in trying to understand her or in respecting her feelings or needs. One therefore has grounds for affording her more compassion than any of the novel's male characters ever do. Yet our final view of her, coldly and companionably plotting with Tom while poor Gatsby lingers outside, is sufficiently distasteful that "[f]ew critics write about [...] [her] without entering the unofficial competition of maligning her character" (Person 1978, 250). Daisy the woman may draw sympathy (along with sexist disparagement), but Daisy the rich debutante-turned full-fledged Buchanan does not.

The book's portrayal of Tom and Daisy amply conforms to *The Rich Boy*'s diagnosis. For example, Tom *tells* Nick "I've got a nice place here," whereas Gatsby *asks* him, "My house looks well, doesn't it?" (Donaldson 2001, 207). When the Buchanans ask Nick whether he is engaged to a "girl out West," he finds their interest so surprising—even as Daisy's cousin and Tom's college classmate—that it "rather touched me and made them less remotely rich," although they remain an object of "disgust[]" due to their other failings.

Thus viewed, Tom and Daisy fall outside the reach of the novel's sympathy—leaving aside Daisy's vulnerability and mistreatment as a woman in a male-dominated society. So when Tom insists at the end that he has suffered too, Nick in effect rolls his eyes, even if he lacks the resolve to refuse the proffered handshake (which itself is just the coda to Tom's being "rid of my provincial squeamishness forever").

How should one evaluate Fitzgerald's didactic viewpoint, so clearly expressed in *The Great Gatsby*, regarding how and why the "very rich […] are different from you and me"? Ernest Hemingway famously mocked it, saying in *The Snows of Kilimanjaro* that the rich are different from the rest of us only insofar as they "have more money." He adds that they are dull, repetitious, drink too much, and play too much backgammon. Hemingway accuses Fitzgerald (aka "Julian") of so yearning to view the rich as a "special glamorous race" that he ultimately was "wrecked" by the realization that he was wrong and Hemingway (of course) right.[3]

Hemingway's diagnosis of Fitzgerald seems itself wrong. The view expressed in *The Rich Boy* and *Gatsby* has less to do with keening for "glamour" than with life experiences about which Fitzgerald was quite self-aware. He explained his lifelong "two-cylinder inferiority complex" (Corrigan 2014a, 46) as a consequence of his having grown up as, in turn,

> a poor boy in a rich town; a poor boy in a rich man's school; [and then] a poor boy in a rich man's club at Princeton […]. [Thus] I have never been able to forgive the rich for being rich, and it has colored my entire life and works. (56)

In short, Fitzgerald's viewpoint reflects the experiences of a moderately affluent American (with a particular temperament) whose circumstances, along with his own ambitions, happened to throw him in extensively with people far richer than he was.

The very specificity of these biographical roots sits ill with viewing Fitzgerald's view as to why wealth inequality matters in America—because it triggers unequal degrees of self-confidence—as providing a sufficiently broad and deep answer to the question. Viewing childhood wealth (or its absence) as the master key could also lead to some surprising broader conclusions. For example, if growing up rich versus poor is all that really matters—given how little Gatsby's too late-achieved

---

3 The rich Americans whom Hemingway shows in this unglamorous light, in such stories as Kilimanjaro and The Short, Happy Life of Francis Macomber, are out of their domestic comfort zones, by reason of their traveling in international circles where it is unsurprising that, say, a macho big game hunter could humiliate one of them who is trying to impress a trophy wife.

fortune seems to help him—then inequality's harms might stay fixed even if, for the members of any age cohort, wealth was completely equalized by age 30. This seems unlikely to be true. Alternatively, suppose everyone started out equal, but that extreme material disparities emerged by age 30, by reason of some people's winning, and others' losing, economic "tournaments" that started after college graduation. Surely the resulting inequality would matter a great deal, even if not by *The Rich Boy*'s proposed mechanism of early-acquired unequal self-confidence. *Gatsby* thereby merely offers one set of reasons, among many, why class and wealth differences might matter.

Upward mobility

Gatsby most definitely takes an interest in upward mobility and what we now call the American Dream. As Lisa Corrigan (2014a, 44) puts it: "Whether all our frantic effort is noble or wasted—whether, in short, meritocracy really exists in America—is one of *The Great Gatsby*'s central questions." Here, in contrast to its relatively unnuanced treatment of the rich, it is distinctly Janus-faced.

On the one hand, one could scarcely rise to wealth faster, or seemingly more effortlessly, than Gatsby does. Even his gangster connections do little to harm him, other than when (in the highest social circles) Tom uses them to shame him in front of Daisy. To the crowds at his parties, the surrounding scent of mystery and crime only makes him exotic and fascinating, not someone to shun. We also never get the sense that he is at risk of being killed by rival gangsters. And, while *Gatsby* stereotypes the likes of Wolfsheim as heavily ethnic Jews with thick accents and tiny eyes, it lacks the sense of menace around bootlegging and other organized crime that would become so culturally prominent in, say, the James Cagney/Humphrey Bogart/Edward G. Robinson movies of the 1930s.

Yet Gatsby's profession clearly undermines the optimism about economic opportunity that his success might otherwise seem to validate. "Fitzgerald chose to make [him] a gangster. He could have affirmed the idea of a meritocracy by having Gatsby rise rapidly up the corporate ladder, be a banker or a grocery-store mogul" (Corrigan 2014a, 138). The fact that Gatsby actually is starving on the streets until Meyer Wolfsheim intervenes can support viewing the book's 1920s New York—despite its nouveau riche tier—as, for most people, a "landscape of bleak class-entrapment and dead-end labor, where rich and poor are frozen in polar extremes" (Fitter 1998, 12).

Such a barbed, rather than optimistic, take on Gatsby's career is reinforced by the novel's deliberately paying "curled lip service" to Horatio Alger's naïve success stories (Scharnhorst 1979). In earlier work, Fitzgerald had repeatedly, and generally sarcastically, invoked Alger's work (which had been hugely popular during his adolescence). *Gatsby* itself may deliberately parody Alger's *Jed the Poorhouse Boy* and similar stories. For example, "Alger's hero Jed Gilman, like James Gatz (who shares his initials) meets his Benevolent Patron aboard the Patron's yacht; each one is hired as a kind of personal secretary [...] receives a new suit of clothing [...] [and] changes his name" (Scharnhorst 1979). Only, Gatsby's patron is a "pioneer debauchee" rather than a paragon, and Gatsby is cheated of his bequest rather than getting to live on it.

One way or another, *Gatsby* challenges *both* of the competing narratives that I call egalitarianism and market meritocracy. Under its view of the rich versus the rest of us, differing childhood circumstances plus inheritance crush any prospect that equality could ever be more than an empty phrase. Moreover, even if the talented can get rich, as Gatsby does, his rise fails to validate his success morally given its criminality. Indeed, his main talent, first recognized by Wolfsheim, is simply a capacity to pass among the plebes, if not in higher and more discerning circles, as a "man of fine breeding" (i.e., as plausibly a well-born WASP). Then, as a final blow to the rags-to-riches faith, the book suggests that even getting rich is not success enough, at least if one is as trapped as Gatsby is in yearning for acceptance by those who were born rich.

Race and class

Race features in three main ways in *The Great Gatsby*. First, the narrative casually expresses the era's racism, while offering us no reason to doubt that Nick is speaking for the author. It is dismaying or worse to read, while Gatsby is driving Nick into Manhattan: "[A] limousine passed us, driven by a white chauffeur, in which sat three modish Negroes, two bucks and a girl. I laughed aloud as the yolks of their eyes rolled toward us in haughty rivalry."

The insult here does not come just from the words "bucks," along with the *Birth of a Nation*-style visual "comedy" of the bulging "yolks." It comes also from Nick's enjoyment of Black people's comic uppityness. How droll that these "negroes" should be so "modish" and haughtily rivalrous, as they style past Gatsby's itself garish "circus wagon" in a fast, flashy car that is driven by a White employee, no less.

As for Wolfsheim—literally, "Wolf's Home"—even beyond the rote Jewish stereotyping, "Fitzgerald goes the extra mile to make [him] repellent by endowing him" with hairy nostrils and human molar cufflinks (Rosenbaum 2012). Wolfsheim also, despite showing a touch of human concern for

Gatsby—inadequate, however, to motivate his attending the funeral—is the novel's "symbol of all that is corrupt about America [...]. Meyer Wolfsheim is Scott Fitzgerald's Shylock" (Rosenbaum 2012).

Second, and perhaps slightly mitigating the first aspect, *Gatsby* mocks Tom Buchanan's crude racism, derived from his excited reading of "this man Goddard's" *The Rise of the Colored Empires*, which is closely based on an actual book by the White supremacist Lothrop Stoddard (Michaels 1995, 23). Daisy ridicules Tom for "getting very profound [...] [by] read[ing] deep books with long words in them." One can almost see his lips moving as he reads. Moreover, it is clear that his own frustration and boredom have triggered what Nick calls this "pathetic" departure from his usual "complacency."

Third, *Gatsby* offers an account of how class and race interact in the 1920s New York. Beyond Tom's ranting, his aggressive response to Gatsby's "presumptuous little flirtation" with Daisy reflects his view that it involves miscegenation (Michaels 1995, 46). Gatsby, born James Gatz, is only ambiguously White and possibly Jewish (Pekarofski 2012, 60–65). Moreover, even if "Gatz" is not actually "Katz"—reflecting the same phonetic switch that Wolfsheim makes by saying "gonnegtion" and "Oggsford" (59)—Gatsby is tainted racially by his Jewish gangster associations. In Tom's words, he is not just a "common swindler" but also "one of that bunch that hangs around with Meyer Wolfsheim," and hence effectively Jewish at least by association.

Without its racial element, *Gatsby* might indeed just be, as is often considered, a story about a poor boy who, once he has made good, tries to pretend that he has always been rich. But this is not just a book about knowing which is the salad fork, or that Oxford men don't wear pink suits. Gatsby must "pretend[] to be something he's not" because he and Daisy effectively "belong to different races [...]. Jimmy Gatz isn't quite white enough" (Michaels 2006).

In sum, *Gatsby* thereby combines (1) expressing racism with (2) mocking it, at least when held too vehemently, and (3) depicting how race and class can toxically interact to create impermeable social barriers. As with its treatment of upward mobility, and in contrast to its treatment of the rich, the book shows more than it tells and leaves interpretive space through its ambiguity.

Consumerism

One of *Gatsby*'s most powerful aspects, at least to many modern readers, is its depiction of anomie, boredom, and disconnection amid the frenzied hedonism of its not-so-merrymakers. Nick, at the first Gatsby party that he attends, is on the verge of "get[ting] drunk from sheer embarrassment" at not knowing anyone until he sees Jordan Baker. Later in the evening, a drunk woman starts crying when she tries to sing, sending her eye shadow cascading down her face until suddenly she falls asleep. Meanwhile, "[m]ost of the remaining women were having fights with men said to be their husbands."

To similarly dismal effect, consider the uncomfortable luncheon that the Buchanans host for Nick, Jordan, and Gatsby, leading to Tom's conclusive takedown of Gatsby after they head to New York for even more "fun." Daisy asks: "What'll we do with ourselves this afternoon? [...] and the day after that, and the next thirty years?" Her affair with Gatsby seems as much the product of boredom as of nostalgia, continuing attraction to him, or anger at Tom.

Meanwhile, Nick, belatedly realizing that he has just turned thirty, can see nothing before him but the "portentous, menacing road of a new decade [...] the promise of a decade of loneliness [...] a thinning briefcase of enthusiasm, thinning hair." For Nick, unlike Tom (who had genuinely experienced a great peak in his days as a college football star), it is not as if his receding youth has been so delightful that he mourns its passing on that account. It had merely been a tad less dull and empty than what he sees lying ahead.

The book wisely does not try to tell us just what all these people are so unhappy or discontented about. However, it leaves enough clues to suggest partial answers. For example, the dominant role of manipulative advertising in "develop[ing] and promot[ing] a new cult of glamour"—extensively on view in *Gatsby*—may leave its hapless targets feeling all the more entrapped in "terminal drudgery" as its "ecstatic" promises remain unfulfilled (Fitter 1998, 2).

Gatsby also amply, and perhaps consciously on Fitzgerald's part, illustrates Thorstein Veblen's famous analysis of pecuniary emulation and conspicuous consumption (Canterbery 1999, 300; Donaldson 2001, 202–3). As Veblen (1899, 31, 32) had explained in his classic late Gilded Age work:

> [T]he end sought by accumulation is to rank high in comparison with the rest of the community [...]. [Anyone below the average level] will live in chronic dissatisfaction with his present lot; [...] [but even after reaching it] this chronic dissatisfaction will give place to a restless straining to place a wider and ever-widening pecuniary interval between himself and this average standard. The invidious comparison can never become so favourable to the individual making it that he would not gladly rate himself still higher relatively to his competitors.

Gatsby's struggles give us a picture of how this anxious, joyless process can work even near the top. Daisy, who as his wife would have been the ultimate luxury accoutrement (Canterbery 1999, 300), proves unavailable for purchase. His status strivings are further undermined by inherited wealth's remaining more honorific than that which is self-earned (in keeping with Veblen's Gilded Age analysis), and by the detailed cultural knowledge that one needs to present oneself convincingly as a member of the leisure class (Donaldson 2001, 202–3).

In sum, both the poisonous lure of advertising and the frustrations around pecuniary emulation offer compelling, textually supportable explanations for the malaise that *Gatsby* evokes. Yet they do not exhaust its interpretive significance, which remains open-ended. Readers in different eras have interpreted the malaise in multiple ways, reflecting the license that the text affords them and eventually adding to *Gatsby*'s cultural resonance.

Geography

Gatsby also depicts geographic restlessness of a kind particular to the twentieth century and afterward. By the 1920s, the Western frontier has long since closed, but America's closer connections with Europe, in the aftermath of World War I, help to give New York City the special cultural place that it has held ever since.

Nick notes near the end that "Tom and Gatsby, Daisy and Jordan and I, were all Westerners, and perhaps we possessed some deficiency in common which made us subtly unadaptable to Eastern life." Yet they all had been drawn to it—in Nick's case, reflecting that, after World War I, "the Middle West now seemed like the ragged edge of the universe." His return home betokens, not a rethinking of the East's superiority to the "bored, sprawling swollen towns beyond the Ohio," but a surrender to that boredom.

Economic boom times

Despite *Gatsby*'s strong flavors of pessimism and unease, it shows clear signs of its having been written in a boom period, when excitement and animal spirits were high. By way of contrast, consider Nathanael West's *The Day of the Locust*— published in 1939, after 10 years of the Great Depression, and also sometimes viewed as a harsh deconstruction of the American Dream. *Gatsby*'s pessimism never approaches *Locust*'s bleakness of tone throughout, nor does its disconsolate ending aim for the apocalypse conveyed by *Locust*'s closing riot. *Gatsby* is dark only to a degree, offering gloom against a bright background.

Gatsby's Initial Commercial Failure and Subsequent Disappearance

A *"flop"* in the 1920s

By the time he published *Gatsby*, Fitzgerald was a prominent Jazz Age chronicler. His two prior novels, *This Side of Paradise* and *The Beautiful and Damned*, had each sold more than 50,000 copies. Knowing that *Gatsby* was his best work yet, he hoped to sell at least 80,000 in the first year (Corrigan 2014a, 205). Instead, it sank so rapidly, along the way to barely over 20,000 sales, that by May 1925, he had concluded it was a "flop" and "isn't going to sell" (207).

This failure was not the product of inattention. *Gatsby* received extensive newspaper reviews, which ranged from hostile to strongly supportive. The most frequent complaint, in a sampling of some lead instances (see Lacey 2013), appears to be that it is just too dark and glum. His characters exhibit "incredible stupidity" and "glittering swinishness" (according to H. L. Mencken's contemporary review). They forfeit sympathy through their "meanness of spirit" and are "dumb in their insensate selfishness." The book is "tired and cynical" and "full of really very unpleasant characters."

A second complaint is that the book is just too short: a "glorified anecdote" (Mencken again) or merely a "thin novel." Also, Fitzgerald's appointed role as the "philosopher of the flapper" has perhaps grown overfamiliar. He is no longer fresh news.

Looking at the novel's main themes as discussed above, the lack of contemporary popular (as well as critical) enthusiasm becomes even easier to understand. The 1920s was not a populist era in which attacks on the rich much resonated. Moreover, *Gatsby*'s cynicism about Horatio Alger success stories was perhaps not even titillating at a time when Alger's sales and readership were rapidly falling (Scharnhorst 1979). Its portrayal of dispirited consumer ennui may have lacked commercial appeal, even among those whom the diagnosis fit. Only with time would some of *Gatsby*'s drawbacks, from the standpoint of popularity, turn into strengths.

Commercial disappearance in the 1930s

Gatsby had sunk from view by the onset of the Great Depression, and hard times' persistence did nothing at first to revive it. The era's "proletarian critics [...] [thought] that all [Fitzgerald] wrote about were the beautiful people buoyed up on bootlegged champagne bubbles" (Corrigan 2014a, 35)—topics that lacked current interest. Wrote critic Philip Rahv, in a review of Fitzgerald's next novel, *Tender Is the Night*: "Dear Mr. Fitzgerald, You can't hide from a hurricane under a beach umbrella." Even the potential populist appeal of *Gatsby*'s attacking the rich seems to have foundered under the burden of its expressing unfashionable fascination with them.

The 1930s were also just too soon for 1920s nostalgia to stimulate public interest in the book. Fondness for a vanished era often seems to need more than a decade's gestation. Thus, consider 1950s nostalgia—epitomized, for example, by the hit TV show *Happy Days*, with its leather-jacketed faux biker character, the Fonz. Set in Milwaukee in the 1950s, *Happy Days* debuted in 1974 and was a breakout hit by mid-decade. Or consider those supreme 1960s icons, the Beatles. They "seemed more *over* [in the 1970s] than they do now, further away than they'd ever seem again" (Sheffield 2017, 263). Only in the mid-1980s, and then even more explosively in the 1990s, did they fully regain their towering cultural standing (295).

Gatsby's revival required a similar time lag. Once enough time had passed, the 1920s nostalgia served as an important trigger. It was not, however, the only one.

The *Gatsby* Revival, 1945–1960

Gatsby's rise to prominence, starting in the mid-1940s, spanned both its popular and its critical standing. The causes of its popular revival are simpler and more straightforward than its critical ascent, even if, in retrospect, neither ought to have been a surprise.

Gatsby's *popular rise*

A key first step for *Gatsby*'s finding a popular audience was the creation, during World War II, of a program to send millions of free Armed Services Edition (ASE) books, printed cheaply in paperback, to American soldiers who were stationed abroad. In 1945, after Germany and Japan had surrendered but well before mass demobilization was imminent, the program sent out 155,000 copies of *Gatsby* (Corrigan 2014a, 236).

ASE books were sufficiently popular with their "[b]ored and homesick" soldier audience that, on average, they were passed around to seven users per book. *Gatsby* may therefore conceivably have had more than a million ASE readers, vastly exceeding its prior reach to any audience (Gash 2015).

The ASE book cover for *Gatsby* adverted both to its "well-remembered" Jazz Age setting and to what Maureen Corrigan (2014a, 236) calls its "bullets and booze" character. Soldiers who started it with this background in mind may have then been "baffled" by "Nick's elegiac opening words," as well as by much of the ensuing poetry and symbolism (236). Yet there was also plenty of raw meat to keep them interested. *Gatsby*, after all, features a potent mix of "bootlegging, crime, [and] explicit sexuality," not to mention three violent deaths (Corrigan 2014b). In addition, consider its precociously film noir-like structure—what with its often-seedy settings, the "fated feel" of its doom-laden trajectory, and its presentation through voiceover narrative (Corrigan 2014a, 10). All this may have helped to make it seem more natural and familiar, as a matter of genre, to readers in 1945 than it had in 1925.

Gatsby's brevity also may have appealed more to 1945 readers of a free book than it had to prospective purchasers in 1925. For either a free or cheap book—including, not just ASE books, but the mass market paperbacks that started appearing in bulk after World War II—large size may chiefly convey the threat of a burdensome reading commitment, rather than the promise of good value for money that matters for a costlier hardcover purchase. For *Gatsby*, therefore, a weakness, from a readership and sales standpoint, had been converted into a strength.

As the postwar paperback boom emerged, new domestic editions of *Gatsby* began "popping up like toasters" (Lucey 2013). A 1949 film version, treating it as an "underworld crime saga" with a noir sensibility (Corrigan 2014a, 131), offers a hint regarding the initial nature of its mass appeal. Only later, as it increasingly became assigned school reading, rather than voluntarily chosen escapism, would this aspect of the story recede relative to its being a doomed love story involving rich people, loaded with overt symbolism that one's teachers might tediously unpack.

Gatsby's critical rise

Fitzgerald's and *Gatsby*'s critical revival in the 1940s, following his death and pushed forward by such prominent admirers as Edmund Wilson (1941) and Lionel Trilling (1945), was almost bound to happen. The book's quality, Fitzgerald's prominence and connections in literary circles, and the requisite passage of time all predictably helped. Less foreordained, however, was the particular form that the *Gatsby* revival took.

At a time when the United States had newly emerged as a dominant and outward-looking world power, the new *Gatsby* criticism focused from the start on the idea that Jay Gatsby is a "symbol of" or "stand[s] for America itself" (Trilling 1945; Troy 1945). More specifically, both William Troy and Lionel Trilling—prominent literary critics who were *Gatsby*'s two first revivalists—described its title character as symbolizing the American Dream.

Maureen Corrigan (2014, 219) suggests that, at a "time of Cold War calcification, when intellectuals are being asked whether they are on the side of America or its Soviet foe," *Gatsby*'s "American qualities [...] somehow resonated." This is not, however, to say that critics who engaged with the book on this basis were looking for patriotic braying. To the contrary, they lauded *Gatsby* for what they took to be its harsh criticism of America. But the nature of the assumed criticism was itself highly flattering. It involved viewing American culture as thrillingly unique in its naïve hopefulness and idealism, even if to be (whether excitedly or mournfully) exposed as misguided and corrupt.

The American Dream school of *Gatsby* literary critics saw the book as supporting a view of America as a country that both needs and has a distinctive great literature, in which we criticize ourselves for national failings that reflect our extraordinary national origins, stemming from the first European settlements and the settlers' centuries-long westward march. America itself becomes a kind of tragic hero, brought low—but only metaphorically, as in a practical sense it was thriving—by its tragic flaws. Thus, as America's economy boomed, and its network of alliances stood triumphantly astride half the globe, the critics' despair (if that is even the word for so comfortable a distress) was like that of a Cicero crying out "O tempora, o mores!" as Rome unchallengeably dominated its Mediterranean world. Deep-rooted self-assurance allows one to be all the more self-lacerating in the realms of morality, happiness, and wisdom.

During the 10-plus years after Troy (1945) and Trilling (1945) first emphasized *Gatsby*'s Americanness, and related it to the American Dream, this take grew dominant in the critical literature. Ensuing critical studies asserted, for example:

- *Gatsby* shows the "corruption of [the American] dream in industrial America," as well as the Dream's "universally seductive and perpetually unreal" character (Fussell 1952, 291).
- It offers "some of the severest and closest criticism of the American dream that our literature affords." Its "profound corrective insights [...] embod[y] a criticism of American experience [...] more radical than anything in [Henry] James's [work] [...]. The theme of *Gatsby* is the withering of the American dream" (Bewley 1954, 223).
- *Gatsby*'s "searching critique of American society" implies that the American Dream may be "little more than a thinly veiled nightmare" (Bicknell 1954, 556).

- *Gatsby* is "of course [...] a criticism of the American dream," even if the label "oversimplifi[es]" because, rather than being "only that and nothing more," it also critiques "dream and illusion" more generally (Stallman 1955, 2, 15).
- *Gatsby* "adumbrate[s] the coming tragedy of a nation grown decadent without achieving maturity—a nation that possessed and enjoyed early and in its arrogant assumption of superiority lost sight of the dream that had created it" (Ornstein 1956).

What, however, exactly constitutes the meat of *Gatsby*'s apparently devastating critique of the American Dream? Later, writers find it "not easy to specify what that dream is" for this purpose (Wasiolek 1992, 15). Clearly, however, the critique that the American Dream critics find in *Gatsby* relates to its vaguer manifestations regarding self-realization and personal fulfillment. They decidedly do not view the Dream as focusing just on practical self-advancement, to the exclusion of mystical self-reinvention.

Yet, given how much the American Dream has to do with the hope of getting rich—even if it is not "merely" about that (Adams (1931, 405)—a takedown cannot ignore the argument that actual upward mobility validates it. The main stances that one could take, in response to such an argument, include the following:

(1) *Practical critique:* Suppose that economic opportunity has sufficiently faded that one really cannot make it to the top without the requisite birth, position, or access to capital. Then the American Dream's promise to the aspiring masses is false.

(2) *Cynical critique:* Suppose that success goes to the cutthroat and the dishonest, rather than to those who are honest, intelligent, creative, or hardworking. Then, while there is upward mobility just as the Dream promises, it rewards the wrong people and fosters bad values.

(3) *Hipster critique:* While "hipster" is a modern term—albeit, with roots going back to the 1920s and 1940s—it can be used more broadly to connote a countercultural sensibility that rejects mainstream values, conventional careers, and vulgar, mass-marketed materialism. Thus, at the risk of neologism, one could say that a hipster—or beatnik or hippie—critique of the American Dream involves viewing its quest as deluded, empty, false, anxious, neurotic, and hence bound to be unsatisfying, even if one actually can get rich.

Gatsby itself could reasonably be read as supporting each of the above three critiques of the American Dream. Its title character succeeds economically, but is unable to join the upper class socially, which is all that he cares about. He succeeds through crime, rather than honest enterprise. And his quest is fundamentally deluded in its obsession with an unworthy romantic object and with the goal of restoring yet denying the past. Plus, the book's depiction of pervasive consumer ennui, extending from the bored Daisy Buchanan to the almost inert Nick Carraway, to Gatsby's frantic yet joyless party guests, suggests that the culture cannot satisfy the cravings that its institutions (such as advertising) help to shape.

For the American Dream *Gatsby* scholars of the 1950s, however, it is almost entirely hipster critique. For example:

- Edwin Fussell (1952) lauds *Gatsby*'s "indictment of American philistinism" (296), while praising Fitzgerald's capacity to expose "the corruption of imagination" by "Hollywood sentimentality and meretriciousness" (303).
- John Bicknell (1954) sees a "vision of society [in which] we have only a choice of mindless evils or pathetic follies" (558). Fitzgerald powerfully illustrates the "liberal and radical [...] [social critics'] conviction that contemporary society in its present stage is ruled by a complex of forces destructive of basic human values and subversive of man's vision of the good life" (572).
- Maurice Bewley (1954) revels in the broader critique of American culture that he sees as embodied in Gatsby's personal "immature romanticism," "insecure grasp of social and human values," and "compulsive optimism" (245). These "terrifying deficiencies," which are "inherent in contemporary manifestations of the American vision itself," not only doom Gatsby personally but also raise the "more important question [...] [of] where they have brought America" (245–46).

Such hipster critiques of American culture—however compelling (or not) one may find them—bring to mind the expressions "First World problems" and "White people problems." By analogy, only in a food-secure country do people start complaining that mass-marketed food products ought to taste better, or to be fresher and more nutritious. Primary needs must be taken for granted before secondary complaints command attention.

Suppose upward mobility were wholly impossible—one was either born rich or else condemned to lifelong poverty. Then the question of whether wealth and its pursuit are deeply unsatisfying would not even arise. Upward mobility must be feasible to begin with before people start scoffing at its psychic efficacy.

America in the post-World War II period was experiencing significant economic growth. It also had more widespread upward mobility than we observe today. The Great Depression was decisively over. The GI Bill was helping millions of former servicemen to find better lives than their parents had ever known. Moreover, people's material lives were improving even more than a purely dollars-based measure would have suggested, whether judged by the rise of home ownership, highways, antibiotics, or television. Accordingly, this was not an era when a practical critique of the American Dream, holding that one simply cannot rise economically, would have gained much credence.

Yet the very fact that things were going so well, so far as the practical critique of the American Dream was concerned, was good news for the hipster critique. In a materially optimistic era, it provided a natural vehicle for expressing alienation from the dominant mainstream culture of, say, Eisenhower and big business. (I say "materially optimistic" because the 1950s had other anxieties—concerning, e.g., the threat of nuclear war and the early stages of rising new challenges to racial and gender hierarchy.)

Gatsby does indeed offer a degree of textual support for the hipster critique of the American Dream—albeit, without being so thoroughly lacerating as a work like *The Day of the Locust*. For example, even beyond the agita around Gatsby's false but entrancing vision, consider the book's depiction of pervasive consumer ennui and malaise. Yet the Dream critics were flattening the book's portrait of American social and cultural tensions in an era of economic excitement. Neither its view of the rich as fundamentally different from everyone else nor its multifaceted dabbling in contemporary racial unease received due emphasis in these accounts. These downplayed aspects helped to leave room for *Gatsby* readings to change in the post-iconification era.

Gatsby Today

Changing critical views

Backlash against *Gatsby*'s critical canonization and mass adoption as an assigned school text was bound to emerge, and it soon did. Gary Scrimgeour (1966) offered an early example, in a piece entitled *Against "The Great Gatsby"* that asserted its literary inferiority to Joseph Conrad's *Heart of Darkness* (which likewise employs a first-person narrator who is fascinated by the lead character). Scrimgeour begins by snarking that *Gatsby* is "just good enough, just lyrical enough, just teachable-to-freshmen enough (and more than 'American' enough) for unwary souls to call it a classic" (75). He eventually resurrects its literary worth, but on the ground that the Dream critics have wholly misread it. If Gatsby is merely "a boor, a roughneck, a fraud, a criminal" (78), and his misty dreams are entirely Nick Carraway's deluded invention, it becomes far darker than the Dream critics had realized and rebuts both their and Nick's "sentimental pessimism" (86).

Even when the Dream critics were not being rebutted, however, there was a shift away from sharing their interests. Later accounts of just how *Gatsby* challenges the American Dream tend to interpret the Dream far more narrowly and literally— for example, as simply promising "material success as the reward for honest hard work and enterprise" (Corrigan 2014, 138). Or "Fitzgerald's commentary on the American Dream appears to be this: The people in the middle pay the price for getting mixed up with the people at the top, the people in control" (Johnson 2002, 43). Or the American Dream critics are simply "mistaken" in interpreting it as being about the "romantic gamble," rather than "the main chance [...]. The actual American dream [of practical material self-advancement] [...] is very much about living in reality" (Schudson 2004, 571–72).

This reflected a relocation of cultural criticism. The notion of *Gatsby* as a hipster critique of the American Dream began to seem increasingly mild gruel as academic writing began to accommodate far sharper criticisms of mainstream American culture—for example, as being racist, sexist, and founded on capitalist exploitation. *Gatsby* could now, with textual support, be interpreted as bearing on issues that, during the 1950s, may have lain outside boundaries of polite (and career-compatible) critical discussion. For example:

Race: *Gatsby's* enmeshment in the world of 1920s anti-immigrant racism, and its both expressing and exposing anti-Semitism, began receiving extensive critical attention. Jeffrey Louis Decker (1994, 67–68), for example, argues that *Gatsby's* purported relationship to the American Dream misconstrues what is actually an anti-immigrant nationalist vision with a "Nordic inflection."[4]

Gender: Daisy Buchanan's role, not just as an object for men to possess and a careless smasher of the less privileged, but also as a victim of the society's sexism and that of the men she knows, began receiving more sympathetic attention.[5] Sarah Beebe Fryer (1984), for example, notes how little any of the male characters understand her and emphasizes her honesty and unmet emotional needs.

---

4 For similar critiques, see, e.g., Michaels (2006), Pekarofski (2012), and Schreier (2007).

5 See, e.g., Person (1978) and Fryer (1984).

Sexual identity: *Gatsby*'s hints of ambiguous sexual identity had been noticed early on. For example, Lionel Trilling (1945) refers in passing to the "vaguely homosexual Jordan Baker." Moreover, one can scarcely fail to notice how much more alluring and exciting Nick Carraway seems to find Gatsby than Jordan or his other passing female love interests. Yet this side of the book had been little discussed, presumably reflecting the boundaries of accepted discourse. Indeed, the American Dream critics tended generally to downplay sexuality's importance in the text. Maurice Bewley (1954, 235), for example, sniffs that even the heterosexual love affair between Gatsby and Daisy is "vulgar and specious. It has no possible interest in its own right."

With time, *Gatsby*'s arguably reaching beyond the strictures of conventional heteronormativity began not only to draw more critical attention but also to be extended beyond Nick and Jordan. Thus, Edward Wasiolek (1992, 21) suggests that

Nick loves Gatsby and hates Tom [...] because Gatsby throws a veil of glamor and fateful romance over his displaced homosexuality, while Tom reveals it in a vulgar and irredeemable form [...]. [Tom's] exaggerated masculinity is as much a sign of his homosexuality as is Gatsby's idealism.[6]

Capitalism: The hipster critique of the American Dream questions the value of capitalist striving, but without fundamentally indicting the system. Instead, it wistfully "align[s] the failure of economic and cultural aspiration with a tradition of high metaphysical defeatism" (Fitter 1998, 2). However, while a view of *Gatsby* as more radical than this might have been poorly received during the prime Cold War period after World War II—and does not appear to have occurred to the 1930s Marxist literary critics—it emerged later on. Some now view *Gatsby* as offering a sophisticated Marxist critique of 1920s capitalism, rooted in an understanding of how "commodity fetishism" (Posnock 1984, 206) or the "hegemonic code of glamour" (Fitter 1998, 14) allows an exploitative status quo to retain its ideological grip.

---

6 On *Gatsby*'s departures from depicting conventional heteronormativity, see also, e.g., Fraser (1984) and Froehlich (2010).

Lessened highbrow critical reputation: Despite all these new critical vistas, *Gatsby*'s highbrow literary reputation appears to have declined somewhat in recent decades. Maureen Corrigan (2014, 274) compares its image in leading English departments, where it is considered "somewhat passé," to that of an "American cheese sandwich on Wonder Bread." She notes that, while *Gatsby* is inevitably included in American literature survey courses, Fitzgerald (along with Hemingway) tends not to feature in upper-level seminars with anything like the frequency of such contemporaries as James Joyce, William Faulkner, Gertrude Stein, or even Willa Cather.

This change is probably not just backlash from *Gatsby*'s having become so canonical. The book's being at once accessible rather than abstruse, yet tasteful rather than extreme, along with its self-consciously beautiful and poetic style, and its extensive deployment of carefully worked-out symbolism: none of these is entirely to modern (or postmodern) critical taste. This has had little evident impact, however, on its continued preeminence in popular culture.

The public's new Gatsby *in our Second Gilded Age*

To the general public today, *Gatsby* is famous not just for being famous, but more specifically for being required reading in so many middle and high schools. Its conscripted readers, no less than voluntary ones, may start out with expectations that end up affecting how they read it. In particular, they may know in advance that Jay Gatsby is a rich, handsome, and mysterious figure—almost inevitably played by Leonardo DiCaprio in the 2013 film version, as he had been played by Robert Redford in 1974—who throws fabulous parties. Gatsby parties, after all, have long been a thing culturally, both predating and reenergized by the 2013 film.

In the actual text, Gatsby first appears in this vein, and we only learn later on about his rise from humble origins. However, whether or not popular readers ever chose the book for its American Dream aspects, they are now more likely than ever to view it instead as being primarily a novel about rich people. Even if they end up connecting emotionally with its pessimism and dissatisfaction—relating this, perhaps, to their own adolescent anxieties about what the future might hold—the notion may linger that its chief virtue is it giving us the chance to gaze voyeuristically at the cavortings of the superrich.

Baz Luhrmann's 2013 film version reflects this sense of *Gatsby* as offering an entrancing spectacle to be viewed from the outside, nose pressed against the glass. His film is a "splashy, trashy opera, a wayward, lavishly theatrical celebration of […] emotional and material extravagance" (Scott 2013). It "explod[es] with the kaleidoscopic colors of the bacchanalian scene" (Dimock 2013), "walloping you intentionally and un- with the theme of prodigal waste" (Edelstein 2013). The Gatsby–Daisy romance gets foregrounded even more than in the novel. (For example, it is no longer clear that Nick and Jordan connect romantically.) However, the central romance itself is more a voyeuristic movie convention than a mechanism for direct personal identification, as one views large-screen close-ups of glamorous, beautiful, and famous actors' well-lit faces.

By increasing the relative prominence of *Gatsby*'s appeal to voyeurism, the Luhrmann film downplays its American Dream-questioning aspect. Voyeurism is a stance that can work at least as well for pessimists as optimists about the feasibility of rising economically. After all, one need not deem the uppermost circles potentially permeable in order to enjoy a fantasy visit—whereas questioning whether the rise is worthwhile presupposes its being at least possible.

Gatsby today may indeed predominantly be, in the public mind as in the 2013 film, an amped-up "Lifestyles of the Rich and Famous," set in a glamorous past period that is delightful to visit (and all the more so if, like Lurhmann, one supplements its jazz with contemporary pop and hip-hop). This outcome is ironic, given the book's depiction of consumer ennui, and its attack on the emptiness and "vast carelessness" of the superrich. Yet these casual modern departures from a fully attentive reading of *Gatsby* reflect Fitzgerald's success in doing many different things at once, while often leaving open what it all might mean.

An Ambiguous Messenger

Two topics of primary sociological interest in *The Great Gatsby* are (1) how the superrich relate and compare to other Americans and (2) whether the American Dream of upward economic mobility is interpreted more narrowly or more broadly. The fluctuating relative prominence of these two topics in reader perceptions of *Gatsby* sheds light on prevailing cultural interests in different eras. However, *Gatsby*'s reception across time also shows elements of cultural continuity.

The superrich

While *Gatsby* is often allusive and subject to multiple interpretations, its view of those who were born to great wealth verges on the didactic, reflecting beliefs that Fitzgerald spelled out at about the same time (in *The Rich Boy*) and that were rooted in his personal life experiences. Reducing wealth's sociological significance to how, when enjoyed from childhood, it affects self-confidence seems both simplistic and reductionist. Moreover, within the novel itself we see rising new alternative elites whose members may care less than Gatsby does about the Social Register class of rich people.

Despite high-end inequality's substantial rise over the last few decades, *Gatsby*'s particular critique of rich people may have resonated more during the era of its postwar reputational rise than in today's post-iconification period. Members of the old WASP/Ivy League social elites—that is, people like Tom Buchanan, apart from his being a Chicagoan rather than a New Englander— were more socially and culturally dominant in the 1950s America than they are today. The early post-World War II period also predated the full transformation from viewing inherited wealth as the most honorific kind (as in Veblen's Gilded Age writing) to today's norm, under which earning a billion dollars is so much more admired than inheriting it that even people who were born to huge fortunes like to pretend they are self-made. In today's world, even a shady self-made criminal like Gatsby might enjoy a status advantage of a sort over a Tom Buchanan, unless Tom's college football stardom came to his rescue.

What may have resonated comparably in all the different periods, however (apart, perhaps, from the 1930s), is *Gatsby*'s treating rich people, including its title character, as objects of an intense fascination that is mingled with resentment. Egalitarian sentiments are not much directly in evidence throughout *Gatsby*, reflecting its Gilded Age-like character and Fitzgerald's focus on the rich. Yet the democratic pretense of broad social equality, at least among Whites, and the lack of a settled model for vertical hierarchical interactions help contribute to the book's pervasive sense of unease.

Upward mobility and the American Dream

Gatsby is not as centrally focused on upward mobility, or the American Dream as interpreted narrowly to denote achieving "merely material plenty," as its reputation sometimes suggests. Again, we meet Gatsby as a mysterious plutocrat many pages before we hear his life story. Even Nick's early expressions of fealty to Gatsby, which tell us that he is not just a plutocrat, turn on his vision, not his rise. Mere economic striving has also been left far behind once one gets to the famous closing, with its orgastic future and boats beating against the current.

That closing can help support reading *Gatsby* as a critique of the broader American Dream, if interpreted as being about finding meaning and self-fulfillment through self-application and self-improvement. Yet *Gatsby* also may not endorse simply finding an off-ramp. After all, Nick's final escape back to the Midwest seems poised to offer him no more than a life of boredom and melancholy nostalgia.

The book also examines racial tensions amid the contested boundaries of Whiteness. It depicts consumerism as frenetic yet joyless, for reasons that may relate both to the lure of manipulative advertising and the impulse to engage in competitive display. It explores geographical unrootedness, what with a narrator who, by the end, can neither abide New York nor imagine finding stimulation elsewhere. And it dramatizes the tensions between vast economic inequality and the cultural presumption that at least all White people are socially equals.

Again, however, *Gatsby*'s diagnosis of American social dysfunction, while broadly suggestive, is deliberately left ambiguous and underspecified, other than in its distaste for the rich. And even that aspect is mingled with a fascination that encourages reading about the book's rich characters in a spirit of voyeurism, rather than just exposé. Thus, while one can readily find a harsh critique of American culture in *Gatsby*, the exact content of which is unclear, one also can just sit back and enjoy the ride.

CHAPTER 4

BAILEY VERSUS BELFORT: COMPARING IT'S A WONDERFUL LIFE AND THE WOLF OF WALL STREET

The Middle versus the Rich and the Poor

Layers of a sandwich

As Ezra Klein has noted, "[t]here is no one group of Americans as revered by politicians and pundits as 'the middle class.' Pity, then, that no one actually knows who is in the middle class" (Klein 2015), or indeed "quite what it is" (Leary 2019). This should come as no surprise, however, in a country in which people well above the 90th percentile consider themselves middle class (Noah 2012, 145) and in which perceived membership requires only that you see yourself as above "the poor" but below "the rich."

In short, the notion that being "middle class" implies some degree of proximity to the middle in wealth or income, however plausible semantically, departs from popular usage. Such usage has more in common with the notion of a sandwich, in which the middle, be it thick or thin, is defined by its distinctness from the surrounding bread layers.

A true sandwich, of course, actually has separate layers, made of distinct materials, whereas the boundaries between classes may be gradual and indistinct, with wealth and income varying relatively continuously. However, one's sense of belonging to a distinctive middle social layer may be sharpened both by focusing on those who are quite distant from oneself—without worrying too much about the exact breakpoints—and by one's awareness of class-associated attributes, such as those pertaining to race, ethnicity, or cultural practices.

Viewing oneself as middle class, based on considering both the rich and the poor distinct Others, invites viewing one or both of those Others negatively. As we saw in the prior two chapters, negative American cultural perceptions of both the rich and the poor have long taken familiar forms. The rich are arrogant, greedy, dishonest, and predatory. And/or, the poor are lazy, stupid, irresponsible, wholly to blame for their own failures, and eager to sponge off others.

While both critiques are familiar, those in the middle need not comparably adopt both. Taking sides primarily against either the rich or the poor, with the other being considered an ally that merits sympathy or even admiration, is a long-standing American tradition. It can help to determine, or else be determined by, whether one stands politically on the left (like Fitzgerald) or on the right (like Conwell and Rand).

The 1930s versus the current era

The divide between those on the left who are more anti-rich and those on the right who are more anti-poor is common to multiple eras. Yet the center of gravity between the two sides can migrate substantially—culturally as well as with respect to political power. For example, the Great Depression era of the 1930s was notably more left-leaning than the current era, at least prior to 2020's COVID-19 pandemic and emerging pushback against racism.

As case in point, consider the following two examples of taking sides between the rich and the poor—each reflecting the broader tenor of its era, despite its being contemporaneously contested:

- In 1936, Franklin Roosevelt, in a major reelection campaign speech, described the wealthy proponents of "Government by organized money" as "unanimous in their hate for me—and I welcome their hatred." As for the poor, in his 1937 inaugural address, he said that "[t]he test of our progress […] [is] whether we provide enough for those who have too little."
- In 2012, Mitt Romney, speaking (he thought privately) to wealthy supporters during his presidential campaign, denounced the "47 percent […] who are dependent upon government, who believe that they are victims […]. [M]y job is not to worry about those people. I'll never convince them they should take personal responsibility and care for their lives." By contrast, Romney publicly urged that "job creators" and "business creators" get the deference and admiration that they deserved. "To say that Steve Jobs didn't build Apple [given the government's role], that Henry Ford didn't build Ford Motors, that Papa John didn't build Papa John Pizza […]. To say something like that, it's not just foolishness. It's insulting to every entrepreneur, every innovator in America."

While Roosevelt and Romney stood, respectively, on the left and the right politically, each was an establishment figure, situated well within the contemporary political mainstream. Thus, each was reflecting the weight of contemporary sentiment in putting his hostility to the disfavored Other as strongly as he did.

Consider first 2012, when Romney spoke. At that time, it would have been hard to imagine a mainstream Democratic politician portraying the rich (as Roosevelt did) as a sinister force whose hatred he actively welcomed. Indeed, President Obama, campaigning for reelection, largely confined his anti-rich rhetoric to criticizing "tax breaks for millionaires" and "ask[ing] the wealthiest households to pay higher taxes." Meanwhile, his supposed disrespect for entrepreneurs and innovators had merely involved his suggesting that they had gotten "some help," including through the creation of "this unbelievable American system […] that allowed you to thrive." He further amplified this mild disparagement by noting that "[t]here are a lot of smart people out there […]. [t]here are a whole bunch of hardworking people," not all of whom had gotten rich. In sum, the rich whom he was critiquing, rather than being enemies whose hatred he would welcome, were merely less exceptional than Randian rhetoric would have had it, and were contributing too little fiscally.

Now consider 1936, when Roosevelt spoke. Republican presidential candidate Alf Landon, in his convention speech, approached the poor far more sympathetically than Romney would decades later. While citing "[t]he law of this world […] that man shall eat bread by the sweat of his brow," Landon accepted that "[t]he whole American people want to work at full time and at full pay," and that "caring for the unemployed until recovery is attained […] is a matter of plain duty." People had lost their jobs and savings due to "economic forces over which they had no control"—not due to their own personal failings. Recovery, moreover, required restoring the confidence of "the small business man […] the average American," as opposed to resting on the efforts (and unshackling) of great business leaders.

It is easy to account for the poor's attracting greater sympathy in 1936 than 2012. The Great Depression, by immiserating millions, had brought poverty close to the door even for millions more who (at least so far) had themselves managed to avoid it. One might have relatives, friends, or neighbors who had lost badly and fear that this would happen soon to oneself. The scale of the economic collapse had also discredited using the long-familiar rhetoric of personal blame to explain millions of people's hardships.

However, the other side of the coin—greater hostility to the rich in 1936 than 2012—is, in at least one respect, paradoxical. During the Great Depression, high-end inequality actually declined in the United States, as the rich lost relative—not just absolute—ground, due to declining asset values (Piketty and Saez 2004). In short, there was a degree of leveling at the top, even though measures of *aggregate* inequality showed an increase because, toward the bottom, so many millions of people were plunging downward.

Recent decades, by contrast, have witnessed very substantial wealth gains at the very top. By one recent measure, since the late 1970s, the top 0.1 percent's wealth share has more than tripled (Saez and Zucman 2014). Meanwhile, as I have noted elsewhere, "the top 0.01 percent was pulling away from the top 0.1 percent, and the top 0.001 percent from the top 0.01 percent, in a process that economists call 'fractal inequality'" (Shaviro 2020, 3).

All else equal, one might expect relative decline at the top to weaken, not strengthen, animus toward the rich. It might lessen, not just their political clout (and hence the anger, inducing power of "organized money") but also the degree to which they inspired resentment and estrangement. To be sure, as we will see, a number of plausible explanations for the seeming paradox come readily to mind.[1] Yet the disparity between the two eras, evidently reflecting causes apart from just the level and trend of high-end inequality, supports the value of taking a closer cultural look at views of the rich and the poor in the Depression era as compared to the current one, including through case studies.

In this chapter, I do so by examining two classic films that span the divide. The first is Frank Capra's *It's a Wonderful Life* (1946), a film which, despite its post–World War II creation and release date, is largely attitudinally rooted in the 1930s—albeit, as we will see, with overlays, reflecting its own decade, that complicate its perspective. The second is Martin Scorsese's *The Wolf of Wall Street* (2013), a biopic based on lead character Jordan Belfort's eponymous (and possibly exaggerated or fictionalized) memoir.[2] *Wolf* is set mainly in the late 1980s and 1990s, but looks back at those years from a twenty-first century perspective that is shaped by multiple public exposures of business chicanery, ranging from the 2001 Enron scandal to the misbehaviors that helped trigger the 2007–2009 Great Recession.

---

1 For example, when capitalist enterprise as a whole seems to be floundering as in 1936, rather than flourishing as in 2012, this itself may put the rich (as the system's main beneficiaries) in a bad light. Moreover, voyeuristic fascination with the rich may be strongest when they are doing well.

2 As *The Wolf of Wall Street*'s screenwriter, Terence Winter, put it, in both the book and the movie, "[y]ou are being sold the Jordan Belfort story by Jordan Belfort, and he is a very unreliable narrator." See Spitznagel (2013).

Commonalities between It's a Wonderful Life *and* The Wolf of Wall Street

The above comparison might initially seem to make for a distinctly odd-couple pairing. After all, *It's a Wonderful Life* is a beloved Christmas-time family film, rooted in fantasy with its whimsically presented angels and miraculous happy ending. *The Wolf of Wall Street* is based on actual events, and largely realistic in style—albeit, depicting extreme behavior in a spirit of black comedy. It was rated "R" for its "strong sexual content, graphic nudity, drug use and language throughout, and [...] violence." *Wonderful Life* embraces idealism, while *Wolf* is pervasively cynical. *Wonderful Life* is set claustrophobically in an almost implausibly "Norman-Rockwellish" small town (Agee 1947), whereas *Wolf* breezily traverses New York City, suburban Long Island, and such global jet set destinations as Miami, London, Switzerland, and the Mediterranean.

Upon a closer look, however, the two films have extensive and even startling commonalities that aid using them as devices for comparing their distinct eras. Their parallels and interrelationships include the following:

(1) Each follows the career of a young man—George Bailey in *Wonderful Life*, and Jordan Belfort in *Wolf*—who was born into the middle class (but not its higher reaches), craves something far better, and is willing to work for it. By the time he is age 12, George is already working for the town druggist, Mr. Gower, to the incredulity of his friends, and first expresses the wish that he had a million dollars, the equivalent of almost $15 million today. Jordan is selling lemonade at age 7, ices on the beach at age 13, and Amway products at age 18, on his way to earning $49 million in a single year by the time he is 26.

(2) Each of these young men is extraordinarily able, standing out markedly from those around him. In *Wonderful Life*, the rich and evil Mr. Potter accurately calls George "an intelligent, smart, ambitious young man [...] the smartest one of the crowd"—as well as the only person in town (besides Potter himself) to keep his head during the Great Depression. Jordan is so gifted a salesman and con man that he mesmerizes a room full of phone marketers within moments of starting his new job at the Investor's Center, and subsequently can even train his loser friends—a bunch of "absolute morons"—to apply his dark sales arts via a script. "Give me them young, hungry, and stupid and in no time, I'll make 'em rich."

(3) Both Bailey and Belfort choose careers in finance that will dominate their lives. George becomes a local banker who fundamentally reshapes the local real estate market by creating the Bailey Park subdivision, filled with single-family homes. Jordan rides the modern stock-trading craze to make Stratton Oakmont a wild overnight success.

(4) Both Bailey and Belfort are inadvertently sabotaged by incompetent business associates. George faces arrest by reason of his idiot Uncle Billy's misplacing $8,000 (more than $100,000 in today's dollars). Jordan, already under federal investigation, has underlings who draw unhelpful police attention by engaging in a public brawl while engaged in money-laundering and later sees his Swiss banker arrested after stupidly venturing onto U.S. soil.

(5) Both lead characters face professional and personal ruin, centered on the threat of arrest and conviction for financial crimes. Each, as the crisis develops, must consider the price of personal loyalty to colleagues. George briefly blusters that he won't take the fall for Uncle Billy. Jordan wrestles with wearing a wire and ratting out his associates in exchange for a reduced sentence.

(6) Both films offer commentary on Horatio Alger-style versions of the American Dream. George turns his back on pursuing great success by choosing to do what is best for his community and friends, rather than for himself. *Wonderful Life* also makes the "truly subversive point that a man could have so many of the things promised by the American Dream (wife, children, job, friends, house, car) and still be unhappy" (Ray 1985, 192). *Wolf*, meanwhile, is an unabashed, if heavily ironic, rags-to-riches success story in which Jordan actually succeeds twice—the second time, when he restores his fortune as a celebrity motivational speaker, even after enduring a $100 million fine plus asset forfeitures and jail.

(7) Both George and Jordan ponder, at least briefly, their degree of responsibility for the well-being of low-income customers. George repeatedly sacrifices his life aspirations to rescue his small bank—and thus, his friends and neighbors, who need it far more than he does—from the ruin that is threatened by Potter's machinations and their own haplessness. Jordan's first wife asks him if he wouldn't "feel better selling [...] junk to rich people, who can afford to lose the money at least." Jordan responds that he can't, because they're "too smart"—only to start doing so once he realizes that he has been giving them far too much credit.

(8) Both movies cast aspersions on the rich. In *Wonderful Life*, when we first see Mr. Potter in an early flashback, the angel Clarence asks pointedly: "Who's that—a king?" The angel Joseph answers: "That's Henry F. Potter, the richest and meanest man in the county." These two adjectives evidently belong together (Ray 1985, 182). In *Wolf*, Federal Bureau of Investigation (FBI) agent Patrick Denham tells Jordan: "You know, most of the Wall Street jackasses I bust, they were born to the life. Their father was a douchebag before them, and his father before that. But you, you got this way all on your own. Good for you, Jordan."

(9) Both films attribute wealth inequality at least partly to unequally distributed talent and intelligence. Potter presumably was born rich, but also is far more patient, ruthless, far-seeing, and clever than anyone else in the town, apart from George. In *Wolf*, Jordan, for all his foibles, is exceptionally able within his particular calling of conning investors, defrauding the market, and inspiring people to follow him.

(10) Despite depicting radically unequally distributed talent, both films disparage market meritocracy. In *Wonderful Life*, Potter is a vicious exploiter who uses monopoly power to extract, rather than create, wealth, and who is driven as much by malice as greed. Even George's high school friend, Sam Wainwright, who gets rich by making plastics from soybeans—based on an idea he heard from George—is both a war profiteer (Johnston 2018, 30) and a jackass. He is always braying "Hee Haw!" to George, on the basis of a childhood joke that he never outgrows. Meanwhile, in *Wolf*, fraud and exploitation are rampant on Wall Street, and not just inside Stratton Oakmont. Jordan learns during his first day at the storied firm of L. F. Rothschild that his job is to make money for the firm, not for his clients, who are merely rubes to be manipulated. Later, he surely has a point when he complains to Agent Denham: "You know who you should be looking at? Goldman, Lehman Brothers, Merrill."

(11) Both films examine the broader meaning and ethics of business success, along with the tensions between career and family, and between pleasure and responsibility.

(12) Both films acknowledge and explore the allure of psychic release and escape through substance abuse. To be sure, in *Wonderful Life*, this is limited to alcohol, whereas in *Wolf*, Jordan and his colleagues combine heavy drinking with a taste for Quaaludes, cocaine (both powder and crack), Xanax, Ambien, marijuana, and morphine. The films' radically different sexual mores likewise make for an instructive comparison.

(13) As we will see, each film straddles several adjoining eras, complicating one's interpretation of the viewpoints that it shows regarding the rich, the poor, and capitalism.

(14) As we will also see, each film adds further complication by offering up rival normative perspectives between which it declines to choose definitively.

In the remainder of this chapter, I address three main topics with regard to each film. The first is how it views the rich, the second is how it views the poor, and the third is the relationship within it between private morals and public or social morality.

It's a Wonderful Life

Placing the film in context

A Depression era film from 1946?

Why would a film made in 1946 be so attitudinally rooted in the Great Depression? Frank Capra had certainly not ignored World War II, which he spent as a U.S. Army major making morale-building documentary war information films for American troops. He had, however, taken a break from his prewar Hollywood film career, which he hoped to resume amid anxiety about his time away. "Had my kind of filmmaker gone out of style?" (Capra 1971, 411).

Capra could have responded by choosing to be topical—like his colleague William Wyler whose film *The Best Years of Our Lives*, concerning soldiers trying to readapt to civilian life after World War II, proved to be 1946's biggest commercial and critical hit. Instead, however, Capra, "not [being] himself interested in making films about ex-soldiers" (Basinger 1986, 65), sought to revive his 1930s genre of films celebrating the "common man," complete with "a message [that was fit] for the Depression era" (59).

Capra therefore chose, through *It's a Wonderful Life*, to make a film that was based on a short story, called *The Greatest Gift*, that an unknown aspiring writer, Philip Van Doren Stern, had written in 1938. Unable to get the story published, Stern had included it in 200 Christmas cards that he sent out in 1943. This fortuitously brought it to Hollywood's attention and eventually to Capra's attention. The story, befitting its composition date, has clear Depression-era elements that the film significantly expanded.

In the story, George Pratt (rather than Bailey) is an obscure small-town bank clerk who wants to kill himself by jumping off a bridge on Christmas Eve, because

I'm stuck here in this mudhole for life, doing the same dull work day after day. Other men are leading exciting lives, but I—well, I'm just a small-town bank clerk. I never did anything really useful or interesting, and it looks as if I never will. I might just as well be dead. I might better be dead. Sometimes I wish I were. In fact, I wish I'd never been born!

Like George Bailey, Pratt is talked out of suicide by an angel who accosts him at the bridge and prompts him to explore the town as it would be if he had never lived. As in the movie, his brother would have drowned, his bank would have failed, and his wife's life would have been blighted (albeit, here by marrying a lout and having bratty children, rather than by becoming what Clarence calls an "old maid"). Otherwise, however, the town without George seems little different than it was with him, reflecting his professional insignificance. There is no Mr. Potter, no class warfare on view, and no indication that the bank (much less Pratt himself) has played any sort of important economic or social role. Pratt is just an ordinary man who learns that even one so humble as he is can have a positive impact on the lives of those who are closest to him.

The Greatest Gift shows its 1930s provenance—in common with Capra's 1930s films—by asserting about the "common man [...] that, no matter how down he might feel and tough his daily job might be [...] he counted for something" (Basinger 1986, 59). This fit the mood of an era in which "individuals wanted to be reassured, and [...] things were tough all over" (59). It also fits the film that Capra apparently thought he had made, whether or not it fit the one that he actually did make.

According to Capra (1971, 422), *It's a Wonderful Life* defiantly celebrates the common man at the expense of those who might claim to be his superiors. He had not made it for the "oh-so-bored critics, or the oh-so-jaded literati. It was my kind of film for my kind of people." It ostensibly shows that even the "slow of foot or slow of mind" are important, and that *"no man is a failure!"* And it "said to the downtrodden, the pushed-around, the pauper, 'Heads up, fella. No man is poor who has one friend. Three friends and you're filthy rich.'"

While that might make for a good film, it is not *It's a Wonderful Life*. For starters, George's friends are directly at fault (along with Potter) for his being on the bridge and planning to kill himself. Desperately though he has struggled and wanted, since at least age 12, to leave Bedford Falls for good, he has not been able to leave it even for a minute—forced instead, as Potter cruelly but not inaccurately says, to "fritter[] away his life playing nursemaid to a lot of garlic-eaters."

Moreover, unlike George Pratt, George Bailey is *not* a common or ordinary man. Rather, he is a truly exceptional one—so uniquely and immensely gifted that even Potter, with his shrewdness and vastly superior resources, must confess to having long been repeatedly "beaten" by him. George also has not just changed a few lives, as anyone might for those immediately around him. Rather, he has singlehandedly shaped Bedford Falls' development path by creating Bailey Park, staving off its devolution into Pottersville, and personally intervening (through painfully self-denying and unrewarded heroism) to save or positively transform numerous individuals' lives.

A film about a mediocre nobody—rich, however, both in friends and positive impact on those closest to him—would have been in keeping with the spirit of both *The Greatest Gift* and Depression-era discouragement more generally. But what about the film that Capra actually made? Here three elements are worth distinguishing.

First, *It's a Wonderful Life* straightforwardly expands on *The Greatest Gift*'s Depression-era resonance by adding Potter and the movie's class warfare. Joseph McBride (1992, 521) views this aspect of the film as more retrograde than just a 1930s lookback, saying that it "paints the Bailey-Potter conflict in the Manichean rhetorical terms of the Populist Party in the 1890s."[3] Yet such views were hardly unusual in the 1930s, when economic hardship had revived the appeal of condemning "malefactors of great wealth."[4] We will see that *Wonderful Life*'s account, not just of Potter's villainy but also of his business model, fits a Depression-era view of wealth as the product of exploitation and clever manipulation, rather than of either hard work or meeting social needs.

Second, we see George Bailey's fury toward and resentment of all the drab losers around him—his ostensibly cherished "friends," who neither share nor understand his aspirations and who in any crisis are helpless without him. Here, the Depression-era connection is more complicated and speculative. As we will see, however, it plausibly reflects the very bonds of sympathy for the poor that the era's ideology so celebrated.

Third, both the film's brief coverage of the World War II era and its aftermath and its depiction of the "New Capitalist" (Agee 1947) Sam Wainwright bring

---

3 McBride (1992, 523) also notes that *It's a Wonderful Life*'s treats women's roles more regressively than had Capra's 1930s work. For example, Mary Bailey's commitment to house and home sets her apart from the professional women played by Jean Arthur and Barbara Stanwyck in Capra's 1930s films. Kaja Silverman (1992, 64) therefore groups *It's a Wonderful Life* with other post–World War II films that sought to dispel the threat posed to male supremacy by women's labor force participation during World War II.

4 While Theodore Roosevelt coined the phrase "malefactors of great wealth" in a 1907 address, Franklin Delano Roosevelt revived it during his 1936 presidential campaign.

an unmistakably 1940s perspective into the mix. So *Wonderful Life* is not just a time capsule, but has its own internal dialogue between eras, both enriching and diversifying its cultural resonance, and contributing to its extraordinary popularity today.

Still, the significant extent to which *Wonderful Life* embodies a Depression-era worldview may help to explain its mediocre box office showing upon release (Basinger 1986, 59, 65; Johnston 2018, 1). Its first-year revenues tied it only for 26th place among American films (Willian 2006, 4). It also, to Capra's and James Stewart's great disappointment, won no Academy Awards—whereas *The Best Years of Our Lives* won Best Picture, Best Director, and Best Actor (Basinger 1986, 65). By the end of 1947, it, "for all practical purposes, was dead" (67).

Then, like *The Great Gatsby*, it sprang back to life, both commercially and critically, decades after its initial release. An inadvertent copyright lapse in 1974 brought *Wonderful Life* early to the public domain (Cox 2003, 113), allowing TV stations free access that they rapidly learned to exploit by showing it repeatedly every Christmas season. The public responded fervently—leading Capra later to muse: "It's the damnedest thing I've ever seen" (Cox 2006). Critics also, by the 1980s, had begun embracing it as an "all-time masterpiece" (Basinger 1986, 69). Widespread acceptance has not, however, yielded a consensus view of the film's perspective on such topics as social class and the American Dream—reflecting, as I discuss next, its surprising resistance to straightforward interpretation.

The Yin and the Yang

To many viewers, *It's a Wonderful Life* offers a "full gale of sentiment" and an "orgy of sweetness" (see Basinger 1986, 66), thus making it "an enriching, sentimental Christmas favorite not to be missed" (Cox 2006). It has been voted the most inspiring film ever made (Johnston 2018, 1). Yet others view it as "terrifying" (Cox 2006), "asphyxiating" (Jamieson 2008), "almost frighteningly bleak" (Ray 1985, 181), or even as "the cruelest film ever made" (Johnston 2018, 70). As Kaja Silverman (1992, 92) remarks in a slightly different context, "[b]oth sets of critics are of course correct."

This duality is rooted in the film's very premise. It starts with a man on a bridge who is about to commit suicide and ends with his joyous salvation through a heavenly miracle. Moreover, this is the contemplated suicide of a strong, beloved, admirable person—as we learn from the very first words of dialogue, in which we hear people praying for George—rather than its reflecting, say, mental illness or unusual psychic fragility. We gradually learn that George, for nearly 20 years, has been withstanding repeated frustrations, disappointments, and betrayals, before finally snapping under the realistic threat of "bankruptcy and scandal, and prison" that is due entirely to his Uncle Billy's being such a "stupid, silly old fool."

Both the fraught starting point and the at least apparently joyous endpoint require a "delicate balance [...] of dark and light," along with a leavening of "humor, but not so much" as to undermine taking George's plight seriously (Basinger 1986, 4). Things must be dark enough for his despair at the start to shed no ill light on him, and indeed to win our unstinting sympathy, as well as to goose up our delight at his ultimate rescue. Moreover, the very need for heavenly intervention implies that *only* by fanciful means can catastrophe be averted—suggesting that, unless we choose to "believe in slightly absurd angels [...] the film ends, in effect, with the hero's suicide" (Pechter 1971, 129).

Yet there must also be enough hope in the air to justify and even exalt George's struggle, however unfairly costly it may have proven to him personally along the way. He spends nearly 20 years battling Potter, preserving Bedford Falls, and defending the well-being of his family, friends, and neighbors. These aims and those people must be worthy enough that his efforts do not seem misguided or even ridiculous. Likewise, the ending would be less happy if one were too conscious (as one probably should be!) of the possibility that, given all the unresolved challenges and his lifelong hatred of Bedford Falls, "he will be back on the bridge—eventually" (Johnston 2018, 70).

Even so, the pervasiveness of *Wonderful Life*'s dualities goes beyond that required by its premise. Its "irreconcilable contradictions" (Ray 1985, 199) pertain to values across the board, rather than being limited to duly balancing darkness and light. Thus, consider the film's political ambiguity. James Wolcott (1986) called it "the perfect film for the Reagan era." At the time of its release, however, J. Edgar Hoover's FBI concluded that its harsh portrayal of Potter and capitalism made it "Communist propaganda" (Johnston 2018, 3). To this day, some critics find it "essentially reactionary" (McBride 1992, 522) and others "truly subversive" (Ray 1985, 192), even if not consciously or intentionally so.

Likewise, consider how *Wonderful Life* approaches small-town America. To some viewers, Bedford Falls is almost absurdly idyllic and wrapped in a "gauzy Currier-and-Ives veil" (Kamiya 2001), reflecting the film's "central ideological project [...] [of] reaffirm[ing] [...] small-town values" (Wood 2004, 721). Yet George, a hero whose perspective we are encouraged to view with great sympathy, has since childhood found what he calls this "measly, crummy old town" so consistently "suffocating" (Johnston 2018, 9) that "it kills him to live there" (17). Indeed, the script tells us that he is "shocked" to learn that his wife-to-be Mary, after her college years away and with New York within her reach, could possibly have been homesick for it. Even Wolcott (1986) concedes that, if you "peel away the picturesque snows of Bedford Falls," Capra is showing us "a town as petty and stultifying as any that drove Sinclair Lewis to apoplexy."

The film's mix between perspectives from the 1930s and the 1940s also contributes to its internal contradictions—in particular, with respect to the rich. However, the most pervasive source of its dualities is the character of George Bailey himself. Played by James Stewart "forever on the edge of hysteria" (Cohen 2010), his "rage building throughout the film" (Jamieson 2008), George is torn apart by his own internal conflicts—arguably more important than the external conflict with Potter. The war between his "sense of moral responsibility […] and his personal desires for adventure, achievement, and success" (Maland 1980, 141) "pits against each other two distinct, well-matched forms of life and conceptions of the good," between which "peace terms do not exist" (Johnston 2018, 4). Thus, the man who has dedicated his life to rescuing Bedford Falls, which he hates, is also a dedicated family man who becomes engaged to Mary only seconds after shouting "I don't want to get married—ever—to anyone! I want to do what *I* want to do!" and who later exclaims: "You call this a happy family? Why did we have to have all these kids?"

Due to *Wonderful Life*'s internal contradictions and dualities, it repeatedly presents a choice between competing values or viewpoints, neither of which receives the film's full endorsement. One often can call these surface narratives and counter-narratives—defining the former in terms of conventional American values and Capra's expressed intent and the latter as pessimistic rebuttals. The dueling narratives not only conflict with each other but also may otherwise be undermined by aspects of the film that fit neither. As we will see, interest lies not just in the film's internal tensions, but in how they elucidate conflicts and instabilities within American ideology that are not limited to the Great Depression.

View of the rich

A serviceable villain

If one thing in *It's a Wonderful Life* is *not* readily subject to conflicting interpretations or ambiguity, it is the fact of Potter's villainy. No sympathetic viewer of the film could easily disagree that he is irredeemably vicious, albeit enjoyably scenery-chewingly so.[5] George is entirely in accord with his friends and neighbors in despising Potter, although he stands alone in having the courage, patience, and foresight that are needed to keep the old scoundrel in check.

Ambiguity does, however, attach to the question of how Potter's portrayal illuminates the film's broader perspective regarding wealth and rich people generally. Consider the FBI's conclusion at the time that *It's a Wonderful Life* was Communist propaganda. Such a view, once shorn of its hysterical, treason-sniffing outer skin, does indeed identify a viewpoint concerning the rich that the film prominently promulgates and that the film's main surface narrative according to Capra—"Three friends and you're filthy rich"—tries to counter.

Potter is more of an archetype than a distinct individual. While he has a full name—Henry F. Potter—we almost never hear it; he is generally just "Potter." This reflects his having "no more intimate personal identity—no family, friends, or relatives—than that single, stark, unadorned last name would suggest" (Carney 1986, 379). So he is the prototypical banker and rich man in town—portrayed as a malevolent capitalist at war with his fellow citizens—and individualized only by his particular animus for the Baileys.

Unlike his prototype Ebenezer Scrooge, Potter never repents. Indeed, at the end of the film, he seems to have gotten away with stealing $8,000 from the Bailey Building and Loan (B&L), and knowingly bringing false embezzlement charges against George. In addition, while the Baileys psychologize him as "frustrated," "sick," and consumed with hatred of "everybody that has anything that he can't have," we never, as with Scrooge, get to see him from the inside or to pity him for underlying traumas that might explain and even excuse his psychological disfigurement.

Potter therefore, unlike Scrooge, remains a classic one-dimensional melodramatic stage villain. This can influence how audiences respond to him and how one might interpret his thematic significance. Stage villains (and their equivalents in other media), ranging from Iago to Uriah Heep to Snidely Whiplash, are at once a "source of vexation for [the] virtuous characters, yet [...] an unmistakable source of pleasure" for the audience (Taylor 2007, 13). They may attract our "perverse allegiance" (29), or at least our "aware[ness] [...] and appreciat[ion of their] willingness to entertain" us (28), while also commanding admiration of their misapplied gifts. We also can simply enjoy them as dramatic foils for the heroes, without taking too seriously what

---

5 A 2018 blogpost by Daniel Savickas, the Regulatory Policy Manager for the conservative and libertarian organization FreedomWorks, bears the title "Henry Potter is the Undeniable Hero of '*It's a Wonderful Life*.' Savickas admits, however, that to view Potter and his actions favorably one must "reject the anti-market, anti-capitalist narrative pushed by the Baileys."

they purport to stand for. Thus, to enjoy the Emperor Palpatine's screen time in the Star Wars saga, one need not literally believe in the Force or the Dark Side or even be greatly concerned about executive tyranny or war crimes.

Audiences are similarly free to enjoy Potter's villainy as merely an exciting dramatic convention, and to view his antipathy to George primarily in personal, rather than social, terms.[6] This may help to explain *Wonderful Life*'s extraordinary popularity long after the counternarrative's Depression-era view of rich people had lost much of its resonance. Within the film, however, Potter's depiction really is far more than just the equivalent of a McGuffin. He is less campily and fancifully presented than a Palpatine or, for that matter, a Scrooge with his "Bah, humbug!" and pitiful self-deprivation. The film seems to take him seriously and at face value—unlike, say, the angels, whose presence is handled tongue-in-cheek and clearly is not meant literally. Thus, even if modern audiences don't always take Potter's sociological depiction entirely seriously, it supports such propositions as the following:

(1) The rich are enemies of ordinary people, whom they despise as "rabble" and wish to dominate and exploit.

(2) Unregulated capitalism does not lead to free markets in the textbook sense, but to the emergence of concentrated monopoly power that allows for untrammeled economic exploitation, and that can strangle ordinary people's hopes of advancement.

(3) Most people are helpless against exploitation by the rich, reflecting, not just unequally distributed power, but also their own cognitive and emotional limitations. Only if lonely and talented heroes (like Peter and George Bailey) should emerge as their champions, and succeed against the odds in defending them, can they hope to resist effectively.

(4) Being such a hero is financially and psychically costly, rather than offering any significant reward beyond the beneficiaries' generally mute gratitude.

---

6 There is a strange intimacy to Potter's interactions with George—reflected, for example, in his startling grasp of George's unexpressed wounds and wants. In the scene where he offers George a three-year contract, at nearly a tenfold salary increase, to join his own organization in a top managerial role, he calls George a man who "hates his job—who hates the Building and Loan—almost as much as I do." Potter understands how "trapped" George feels, and how humiliated at having to stay behind and "watch his [less capable] friends go places [...]. You wouldn't mind living in the nicest house in town, buying your wife a lot of fine clothes, a couple of business trips to New York a year, maybe once in a while in Europe." All that Potter misses is George's desire to do creative and socially important things.

All this, of course, is not pro-Soviet communism as the FBI blustered to itself, but rather an indigenous 1930s (or 1890s) American populism. Still, its darkness and pessimism, in tension with *Wonderful Life*'s aim of providing emotional uplift, make it a counternarrative, requiring rebuttal. Tellingly, however, the surface narrative to which the film assigns this task, based on the motto "Three friends and you're filthy rich," takes on only the last of the above four propositions. Moreover, even this challenge is not especially effectual.

Rich in friends versus economically rich

On its face, the maxim "Three friends and you're filthy rich" sounds more like encouragement for the humble than disparagement of the great. And in *The Greatest Gift*, from whence Capra derived this theme, encouragement rather than disparagement clearly is the point. The story shows a humble man renouncing despair and suicide once he better grasps his importance to loved ones. Neither rich people nor friends as a rival coinage of true wealth (as distinct from just a source of happiness and contentment) are ever mentioned in it.

In *It's a Wonderful Life*, however, George Bailey's elevation far above the mere "small-town bank clerk" status of George Pratt and the addition of Potter as his prime antagonist convert this focus on friendship from merely an uplifting bromide into a rebuke of rich people's claims to superior status. This is made plain by the only two scenes in the film that expressly mention the idea of wealth in friends.

The first is the Bailey B&L meeting after the death of George's father. Potter, seeking the B&L's liquidation, mocks Peter as "a man of high ideals, so called" that had given rise to a "discontented, lazy rabble instead of a thrifty working class," and that condoned improper favoritism ("if you shoot pool with some employee here, you can come and borrow money"). George, in response, blows up: "People were human beings to him, but to you, a warped, frustrated old man, they're cattle. Well, in my book he died a much richer man than you'll ever be!"

The second mention of friends as true wealth comes at the very end, from George's brother Harry. To the acclaim of all those who have crowded into George's small, packed living room, Harry, ignoring his own central role in consigning George to a life of bitter frustration,[7] cheerily toasts "[t]he richest man in town!" In context, this plaudit unmistakably is a dig at George's antagonist, who everyone knows is literally that.

---

7 Earlier in the film, Harry has repaid George, who heroically rescued him from drowning as a child, by reneging on his own promise to take over the B&L, thereby opening his own path to becoming both rich and a war hero, while his big brother is relegated to becoming (as Sam Wainwright puts it) "old moss-back George."

The competitive rivalry between George and Potter is clear enough that Potter strongly feels it himself. He sufficiently seethes at George's calling him "warped" to throw it back at him 18 years later[8]: "What are you but a warped, frustrated young man? A miserable little clerk, crawling in here on your hands and knees and begging for help." Potter also cannot wholly ignore the weight, if not of personal friendships, then at least of democratic popularity. In the scene where he offers George a job working for him, he volunteers that "most people hate me," although ostensibly the fact that "I don't like them either [...] makes it all even." Despite this protestation, however, we can see that Potter's wealth, unaccompanied as it is by any positive human connections, does not actually make him happy.

Nonetheless, the claim that friendship is more important than wealth—or rather, that those who are rich in friends are superior to those who are merely financially rich—neither captures the film's true case for the Baileys, nor seems to offer them much comfort. As to friends as the supreme coinage, neither George nor Peter Bailey is an especially gregarious type. They both are far too driven and hardworking. Moreover, George is deeply isolated by the lack of anyone in his Bedford Falls social set who shares, or even seems to understand, his aspirations (apart from Mary, who has been set since childhood on blocking their realization).

The true countervalue to wealth, therefore, is not so much having friends as being the people's champion, and thereby earning their gratitude and appreciation. Even as such, however, neither Bailey seems either enviable or happy. Peter has been driven to a premature death by stress, frustration, and hard work, after a life that, as George tells him, seems unbearably "shabby" and small. Then George ends up on the bridge contemplating suicide and can only be saved by a whimsical fantasy of divine intervention.

George, moreover, appears to derive little pleasure from his popularity—however moved he may (temporarily?) be, in the final scene, by his neighbors' support. He repeatedly saves Bedford Falls out of a joyless sense of duty and always at the cost of mortifying self-sacrifice. His own life ideal is highly individualistic. He has wanted to be not just a millionaire by age 30, but a kind of Robert Moses (Johnston 2018, 6), perhaps intermixed with Frank Lloyd Wright, who would get to "build things [...] design new buildings—plan modern cities."

Financial wealth, travel, and luxury—more than popularity, which seems not to figure here—are indeed a central part of what would make George feel subjectively "rich." To be sure, the larger package also embraces importance

---

8 The battle over the B&L's future after Peter Bailey's death takes place in 1928, and the film's denouement occurs in 1946. See Willian (2006, xiv).

and social impact, along with the chance to try one's mettle and use one's imagination (Carney 1986, 388). This added aspect helps to explain why Sam Wainwright's offer of a "ground floor [...] chance of a lifetime" to make a fortune in plastics fails to tempt or even interest him.

Yet a sense of social purpose and moments of pride about having done things that made a positive difference in people's lives are not the same as feeling "filthy rich" so long as you have at least three friends. They also seem inadequate to give George the satisfaction he needs, which would have required his getting to act on a much larger scale. So the surface narrative leaves the Potter counternarrative still in full possession of the field, leaving aside the disparagement that does indeed result from its redefining "richest," with a connotation of "best," in terms of positive impact and public service, rather than just money.

As it happens, however, other aspects of *Wonderful Life* more tellingly modify or undermine the Potter-based counternarrative regarding the rich. These can be divided into internal challenges, or those arising within the Potter story itself, and external challenges, pertaining to what we see from other parts of the film.

Internal challenges to the Potter-based counternarrative

The Potter-based counternarrative depicts the rich as threatening and dangerous, even if one can defiantly invoke the surface narrative to disparage their claims of personal superiority. However, two aspects of Potter's depiction weigh against viewing him with quite as much fear and grudging awe as the counternarrative appears to suggest.

First, we see that his grip on Bedford Falls is potentially fragile. Potter has enough political power that, when a congressman calls in person to see him, he feels free to instruct his secretary: "[T]ell the congressman to wait." Yet the root of his local dominance is economic, and it rests, not just on his having a lot of money, but on the lack of competition in the real estate and lending markets. Hence, the Bailey B&L truly threatens his position, and he is not just pursuing an "obsessive personal vendetta" (McBride 1992, 521) against the Baileys. An aide actually warns Potter that "you can't laugh off this Bailey Park any more," and then muses to himself that "one of these days [...] [I will] be asking George Bailey for a job."

Second, there is no glamor or aura around Potter and his wealth. Instead, he is physically repulsive and evokes disgust. In the "riveting seduction scene" (Johnston 2018, 29) where he seeks to hire George away from the B&L, it is not the job's lack of challenge or social purpose that kills the deal.

George actually agrees to Potter's drawing up the papers, while he will discuss with his wife the possibility of his accepting a nearly 10-fold pay increase along (one suspects) with shorter hours and reduced stress. Only when Potter offers to shake hands does George pull back. What the screenplay calls the "cold mackerel" feel of Potter's hand triggers "physical revulsion" in George, so that he "drops his hand with a shudder." He then clenches his fist, starts to shout, and storms out after calling Potter a "scurvy little spider."

This is not exactly a *Gatsby*-like—or, as we will see, *Wolf of Wall Street*-like—picture of great wealth and its holders as seductive and enticing. Insofar as Potter is a stand-in for rich people generally, it suggests how little they appear to command admiration or awe in a Great Depression setting. His repulsiveness brings to mind the fact that, in the 1930s, the richest Americans were neither personally prospering to the same degree as their peers in other decades, nor garnering comparable prestige from their association with capitalism. Hence, it fits well with the seemingly paradoxical view that animus toward the rich may tend to be stronger when they are sinking, rather than rising.

External challenges to the Potter-based counternarrative

Potter offers only one of the four business models, larger in scale than operating a taxicab or a bar, that are on view in *It's a Wonderful Life*. The other three are the Bailey B&L, the architect career that George envisions for himself outside Bedford Falls, and Sam Wainwright's plastics empire. They show, at a minimum, that Potter's is not the only way of running a business or even of making a lot of money.

(1) *The Bailey B&L:* Under one view of *It's a Wonderful Life*, Capra balances the slate by contrasting the bad businessman, Mr. Potter, with the good ones, Peter and George Bailey. This ostensibly shows that "the power of money can be used oppressively and it can be used benevolently" (McBride 1992, 517). However, while it is true enough that the Baileys are private sector heroes—the film does not explore political responses to Potter (who owns the local Congressman)—George agrees with Potter that "my father was no *business* man." Moreover, however noble and commendable we may find both Baileys' community service, a business in which the owner doesn't "ma[k]e a dime," and cannot even fund his children's college educations, hardly seems to offer a feasible rival business model, much less suggest that one can get rich ethically. Indeed, the film's depiction of the Bailey B&L seems to raise the possibility that *any* significant profit for the lender is inconsistent with helping people.

(2) *George's forgone architect career:* George's idea of becoming a Robert Moses
or Frank Lloyd Wright, and making a million dollars by age 30 while also
helping to shape modern urban life in a positive way, appears to have
more promise as a business model to rival Potter's. While we do not know
if George could actually have achieved this, there is no indication that
it is just fantasy. Yet, presumably, only a person of great ability—like
George himself, but almost no one else in Bedford Falls—would have a
good chance of getting rich this way. George's eagerness to embrace this
path does, however, suggest that one can achieve deserved wealth through
productive business activity that actually benefits people. The lack of any
such opportunities in Bedford Falls might say more about the limitations
of small-town America than of capitalism.

(3) *Sam Wainwright's plastics business:* Sam Wainwright is the one "New
Capitalist" we see in *It's a Wonderful Life*—unless we also count George's
brother Harry, whose father-in-law recognizes his "genius" as a researcher
in the glass business once Harry has married the man's daughter. If one
person should be "imaginatively disturbing" to George, it is indeed Sam.
"He is a millionaire world-traveler and industrialist who lives the dreams
of travel, glamour, romance, and wealth about which George only reads
and dreams" (Carney 1986, 385).

Yet "should be" does not seem to add up to "is." George finds Sam such a braying
and trivial lightweight that envy never seems to figure in their relationship. Even
when Mary uses Sam's fortuitous phone call, right when George is visiting,
to crash through George's ambivalence about her, the thought of Sam as a
romantic rival appears to carry less weight than the couple's sheer physical
proximity while they share the phone.

Sam's slightness as any sort of a counterweight epitomizes *Wonderful Life's*
retaining a predominantly Depression-era mindset, even as it displays evidence
of its post–World War II provenance. With historical hindsight, however, we
can see Sam as the forerunner of people who would help transform the image
of the rich from Potter's repulsiveness to something far more glamorous and
alluring. The film thereby hints at a future rise in the prestige of the rich that lies
outside its Depression-era mindset.

Summing up

It's a Wonderful Life's hostility to the rich, rooted in Depression-era attitudes,
emerges in several ways. Most obvious is the left-populist counternarrative

that emerges so clearly (and indeed didactically) from its depiction of Potter. The bleakness of that view appears to help motivate the film's putatively upbeat, albeit far from entirely convincing, surface narrative to the effect that friendship and human connection make one richer than money ever could—a theme that it repurposes from *The Greatest Gift*, where it is merely uplift for the humble, to make the case that the Baileys, father and son, are better than Potter.

Meanwhile, Potter's sheer physical repulsiveness conveys a sense of the Depression-era rich as lacking the seductive glamor of a Jay Gatsby or a Daisy Buchanan. Sam Wainwright's seemingly enviable (if shallow) jet-setting lifestyle offers us a hint that this might be about to change, but both the film and George view him with too little respect for this to be currently actualized.

View of the poor

Wonderful Life's internal debate concerning the poor is laid out during the battle over Potter's motion to shutter the Bailey B&L after Peter's death. Again, Potter, posing the counternarrative, complains that Peter's coddling of his clientele with commercially unsound loans, has given Bedford Falls a "discontented, lazy rabble instead of a thrifty working-class." George responds:

> [T]his rabble you're talking about [...] they do most of the working and paying and living and dying in this community. Well, is it too much to have them work and pay and live and die in a couple of decent rooms and a bath?

They are "human beings," not "cattle."

This hardly sounds like an even debate. Potter presents his views almost as repugnantly as Scrooge, when the latter argues that the poor should be allowed to die so as to reduce the "surplus population." George, by contrast, argues for simple decency. Yet two points about Bedford Falls' working poor, as depicted in *It's a Wonderful Life*, prevent this debate from being the sort of boring walkover that one might have expected. The first is that, while the poor surely deserve compassion—and are *not* being spoiled, as Potter asserts, by the Baileys' efforts to rescue them from his exploitation—they also are rather weak and pitiful. If not entirely responsible for their own hardships, given their pressing needs and limited opportunities, they also seem to be almost entirely hapless. Moreover, in the dystopian Pottersville fantasy sequence, we see, not just how poorly they would "turn out [...] if not for George," but also, perhaps, "their venal internal selves stripped bare" (Jamieson 2008). Thus, Uncle Billy goes mad and is institutionalized, the druggist Gower negligently poisons a customer and becomes the town drunk, Violet Bick is a "tart," Ernie the cabdriver is glum and "much harder," Bert the policeman is a "trigger-happy madman" (Jamieson), and Nick the bartender is a "deliberately unpleasant" surly tough guy (Wade 2000). So even their decency and minimal functioning appear to depend entirely on George's help. Otherwise, they might not be much better than Potter's "cattle."

Second, George feels real hatred and resentment of these people, reflecting the sacrifices that their needs have forced on him. When Potter perceptively calls George a man who "hates his job—who hates the Building and Loan—almost as much as I do," it concerns George's needing to "play[] nursemaid to a lot of garlic-eaters"—not loyalty to a particular small financial institution just because it happens to bear the Bailey name. Indeed, if one looks from the outside at how the plebes have affected George's life, one almost seems to get an uncanny advance echo—albeit, coming from a different place—of the Ayn Rand/John Galt critique of the masses who drag down the "Men of Genius" if the latter should be foolish enough to subscribe to altruism.

Given the townsfolks' dependence on George's heroic self-sacrifice, which costs him everything he wants from life (other than the ambivalently embraced Mary), they truly are what Galt might call parasites, if not quite cannibals. Of course, the mechanism is not their directly taking his wealth, as happens (according to Galt and Rand) if there is even a minimal tax-funded welfare state. There also is no dignitary threat here. George, unlike the grandiose Galt, is not hysterically tantrumming about the common folks' lack of due respect for him. Rather, the problem is that they have conscripted his services by appealing irresistibly to his conscience.

This is a distinctively, if not uniquely, Depression-era type of problem to have. The 1930s was a time when the call, both personal and ideological, for solidarity with those less fortunate than oneself could imply a need for real self-sacrifice. In illustration, consider three stories that are drawn from my own family history, but that may, as generalized, have been common at the time:

- The editor of a rising periodical journal quit his job when the staff went on strike, so as not to be a "scab." This left him unemployed in the middle of the Great Depression, with a wife and two children at home. His less scrupulous replacement reportedly used the editorship to launch a lucrative career in publishing.
- A commercial artist who did photo-like paintings for mail catalogs found that his job was secure as the Great Depression deepened, making him

more fortunate than many of his relatives and artist friends. Apparently with great amiability, yet presumably reflecting the expectations he faced within a close-knit community of recent immigrants, he spent years helping to support many others who were in need. As he was far from being actually rich, this may have required significant sacrifice.

– A father with two young children died of pneumonia, leaving the task of household survival on the shoulders of his wife, who had never worked outside the home and who initially spoke no English. Hard though she worked in the face of this challenge, it "took a village," as the saying today goes, to see them through. Family members, neighbors, and friends who were doing well enough pitched in as needed, both financially and otherwise.

On the whole, these are positive stories that suggest the Depression-era strength (at least among immigrants) of extended families, peer solidarity, and communitarian feelings. For the aspiring and successful, however, the ethos that they depict could imply pressure to stay true and close, even at a significant personal cost. An extension might be guilt about achieving success, potentially countered psychologically by one's feeling all the more vehemently that it was indeed deserved, and that others were at fault if they could not match it.

In this respect, consider Capra himself, who came to America from Italy at age 5 (in 1903) as part of a large and desperately poor family that had to live in what he subsequently called the "sleazy Sicilian ghetto of Los Angeles." He begins his memoirs with the words "I hated being poor. Hated being a peasant" (Capra 1971, xiii). Years later, after finding a secure place in Hollywood just in time to weather the Great Depression comfortably, Capra began making films that often used the "prototype [...] of the common man protagonist thrown into a situation of great wealth and tempted to forget his true allegiances" (McBride 1992, 233). This gave him, for many years, a liberal or left-wing reputation, even though he was a lifelong Republican (256–57) whose "Darwinian social beliefs" reflected the view about poor people that, "if he, a poor immigrant boy, could make it to the top, why couldn't they?" (258).

Both sides of this are in display in *It's a Wonderful Life*, despite its all too easy disparagement of Potter for his over-the-top hatred of the poor. Sympathy for the less fortunate and defining decency in terms of helping them bump up against portraying them negatively and dramatizing the suffocating weight of their neediness and inadequacy on a talented young man with entirely reasonable, and indeed laudable, ambitions.

Private morals and social morality

George's clenched-teeth self-sacrifice makes clear the importance of social morality, or obligations toward others, in *It's a Wonderful Life*. However, the film's moral interests extend beyond the social realm to cover private morals as well, pertaining mainly to sexual behavior but also the use of alcohol. The social and private realms appear to be closely linked, and each yields the film's usual unresolved battle between competing narratives.

In both realms, the surface narrative holds that conventional morality is essential. Socially this involves concern for one's neighbors and the poor, while privately it involves heterosexual marriage with children and a traditional home life, along with sobriety (albeit not requiring abstention from alcohol). The counternarrative holds that these values are not just at war with achieving personal satisfaction, but actively and almost maliciously hostile to it.

In effect, one cannot have social justice without vicious self-denial. So both the surface narrative and the counternarrative lead to a place that is intolerable, either in the private realm under the surface narrative or the social one under the counternarrative. These links between the two realms suggest that a more "liberated" society (in our terms), even if predominantly benign in the private realm, may tend to be colder and crueler than Depression-era America in the social realm.

Social morality

Both the surface narrative, extolling concern for the less fortunate and the counternarrative, complaining that the personal cost of helping them is just too high, receive powerful support in *It's a Wonderful Life*. Suppose we agree that traditional Bedford Falls and Bailey Park are much better than Pottersville—although, some commentators (such as Jamieson (2008) and Kamiya (2001)) enjoy questioning this. Or suppose that we instead just focus on the long list of individuals whose lives George saves or positively transforms. Then George, by repeatedly sacrificing the life and career he wanted, has achieved great things. He surely has made things far better overall under any sort of a utilitarian calculus where others' welfare matters as much as his—even without adding in special concern for social justice, preventing exploitation, and aiding the worst-off. Clearly, then, he has consistently done the right and best things.

Yet the costs he bears for doing all this seem as unjust—or even more so—than all the harms that he singlehandedly prevents. His desire, not just to make a million dollars and see the world but also to test himself and achieve great things, could not fit better than it does within the higher reaches of the American Dream, with their focus on greater vistas than just a job, home, and family. Moreover, even if American culture did not so valorize aspiration, it is not founded on cherishing martyrdom or renunciation. Thus, the fact that George's "sacrifice seems in excess of what even a culture predicated on renunciation would demand of its subjects" (Silverman 1992, 99) is unacceptable—not just regrettable—from an American cultural standpoint.

The film goes out of its way to heighten the undeserved cruelty of all George's sacrifices. It is almost like a bad joke how each time he does something especially good, he pays a steep price for it. By reason of saving his brother's life, he goes deaf in one ear (later, requiring him to be "slacker George" in lieu of getting the chance to be a war hero). By reason of saving Gower from drunkenly poisoning a customer, he gets slapped in the head, hurting his bad ear. Later, he can seemingly be moments from leaving town at last, be it for college or his honeymoon—making it seem almost certain that, surely *this* time he will escape—but, fear not, *something* will happen to stop him. The only thing he can ever be sure of is maximum disappointment. And while the film purports to rebut all this with its surface narrative holding that he actually has had a "wonderful life" after all, this is so slapped-on, through the injection of fantasy into an otherwise realistic film, as to "reveal the profound weakness of the cause for which [it tries] to enlist sympathy [...] [and] tacitly discredit what [...] [it] pretend[s] to impart" (Kracauer 2012, 75).

Accordingly, for all the uplift that *It's a Wonderful Life* delivers in its final scene, it portrays what is really an intolerable conflict between social and personal imperatives, neither of which has clear priority. It is too classically American in its individualism to embrace George's sacrifice, but also too communitarian to deem it just too bad for the "garlic-eaters" if they cannot fend for themselves. Meanwhile, its communitarianism, founded on helping the weak, is part of a broader moral code that likewise can neither conquer nor submit to Americans' "unalienable Right[]" (as the Declaration of Independence puts it) to the pursuit of happiness.

Private morals

It's a Wonderful Life's community-based moral values are not, of course, limited to solidarity and helping the weakest. They also embrace conventional American private morality, with young men and women looking for opposite-sex romantic

partners, promptly getting married once they find the right person, and then
having children that they raise together—all the while prudently saving for
homes, nice cars, and the children's college educations.

Somewhat softening the moral code is a good-sized helping of nudge–nudge,
wink–wink joshing about sexual morals. For example, the sympathetically
(if disrespectfully) treated Violet "happily" asks Mary early on what's wrong with
liking every boy. The young George wants a "harem." Later, men ogle Violet
to the point that one almost gets hit by a car, and another promptly announces
that he is rushing home to see his wife. George relishes the "very interesting
situation" where Mary's robe has come off and she is hiding behind a bush—
having just been catcalled by an old man on a porch for not kissing her already.
Still, however, beyond the realm of good, clean fantasy fun, Bedford Falls is
a sufficiently straightlaced place that people stare pointedly at George when
he briefly meets with Violet in his office, allowing Potter, only hours later, to say
it's "all over town that you've been giving money" to her.

Another aspect of the moral code relates to alcohol. Drinking to relax
is presented as normal behavior. When people get too unhappy, however,
they drink too much, and bad things happen. Gower's drunken near
catastrophe results from his response to finding out that the 1918 Spanish
flu has killed his son. George, en route to the bridge, gets drunk because
he needs to anesthetize himself, and crashes his car. In the alternate reality,
not only has Gower become a pitiful alcoholic, but heavy drinking among
stressed-out Pottervillians at Nick's Bar has replaced the more convivial
Bedford Falls ablutions at Martini's.

One could imagine deriving a radical critique of the society's restrictive
moral code from *It's a Wonderful Life*'s depiction both of sexual regimentation
and of the apparent need for alcohol as a safety valve that readily gets out of
hand. That, however, would imply an agenda of personal or social liberation,
based on the importance of pleasure or happiness, that bears little relationship
to the film's main concerns. Instead, the film criticizes the norm commanding
that one marry and settle down—like that commanding that one help the less
fortunate—simply because it ties down the rare extraordinary man who would
rather go off by himself to realize great ambitions. (As Potter puts it in the job
offer scene, George's life and career path through age 28 would be just fine if
he was a "common, ordinary yokel.")

The critique might not be so sharp if George deliberately chose marriage
over his ambitions, having weighed the rival appeal of each. Then he would
merely have learned that one cannot always have it all. Instead, however,
not only is he repeatedly denied the chance to leave, when he could not be

clearer about preferring that course to marriage, but in addition he is somewhat tricked and stampeded by Mary. She wages an aggressive, deceptive multiyear campaign to force George to stay at home with her instead of doing what he wants—causing marriage (at least for George) to look like as bad a trap as his feelings of compassion for the poor.

Mary's campaign starts, at least in conception, when, as a "small girl," several years younger than George (who is 12), she whispers into his deaf ear that she will always love him, just after he has proclaimed that he wants to be an explorer with "a couple of harems and maybe three or four wives." In context, "Mary has issued a [covert] declaration of war against him—on her own behalf, on behalf of Bedford Falls, traditional marriage and family, on behalf of a form of life [...]. [W]hat George wants (or thinks he wants) is irrelevant" (Johnston 2018, 14).

When they reconnect at her high school graduation dance (after she has mutely admired him for years), she sets about trying to make it happen. However, she never levels with him about this—for example, secretly wishing for the future that she then brings about, in front of the house where they will eventually live, even though he has just told her that he wants to leave Bedford Falls for good. She then manipulates him, through their physical proximity during the phone call with Sam that keeps him from storming out of her house, into issuing perhaps "the most anti-romantic proposal in the history of cinematic marriage" (71).

Even after the wedding, the deception continues. While Mary is apparently fine with the long, round-the-world honeymoon that George plans, when asked about what comes next, she says: "After that, who cares?" In fact, she has already bought their new home—which George, 13 years later, will call "[t]his drafty old barn!" Perhaps Mary just wants to preserve the surprise; George knows they are returning to Bedford Falls after the honeymoon. He soon comes to understand, however, that she has pushed him into a life that she knew all along he did not want. He responds by ceasing to "regale [her] with tales of his ambition," which obviously are unwelcome and a mockery now, and by "turn[ing] taciturn—and passive-aggressive" (81). For example, he shares with her neither the rejected job offer from Potter nor the cause of his distress on the night when he heads to the bridge.

This tale of Mary's manipulations could easily support a misogynistic narrative in which she, perhaps standing in for women generally, is the villainous foe of male dreams and achievement. Yet this is not how it comes off, and not just because the two of them truly love each other—if selfishly on Mary's side, and merely as a "consolation prize" (52) on George's—but also because she (despite all this) is simply too sympathetic and even admirable a character. She is by far the most capable, forceful, and intelligent person in the movie, along with the evil Potter and the ever-frustrated George himself.

Mary is the type of person who, at the high school graduation dance, has the good humor to keep on dancing with George even after they have fallen into a swimming pool in full party dress. During World War II, she "had two more babies, but still found time to run the U.S.O." At the end, when in his frustration George starts raging at the children, she has the calm resolve to throw him out of the house. Then she smoothly turns to marshaling the neighbors so as to orchestrate his rescue from jail and disgrace.

While her indifference to his wants may show "a certain cruelty" (19), in other respects she is a paragon. Not far in advance of the first television sitcoms, she epitomizes the middle-class American mid-century housewife, portrayed as calmer, more perceptive, more realistic, and more mature than her mate. She merits criticism solely for not seeing (or at least not caring) that a manner of life, which the film allows us to agree might be good for almost everyone, is not good for George, simply because he is so extraordinary.

*****

Even if George Bailey had not wanted to be an architect—like Howard Roark, the hero of Ayn Rand's *The Fountainhead* (published in 1943)—*It's a Wonderful Life* would have oddly Randian echoes. It could scarcely be less Randian in its hatred and even disgust toward the rich, its veneration (however contemptuous) of the poor, and its accepting the obligations imposed by conventional morality. Yet it lavishes both admiration and empathy on the figure of the extraordinary man who is being unfairly denied self-fulfillment. Only upward-looking disgust, downward-looking sympathy, and the force of conventional moral dictates keep him from actively seeking it, and from embracing his own deeply felt scorn and disgust regarding his "friends." These factors will be long gone when we jump forward 67 years, from the release date of *It's a Wonderful Life* to that of *The Wolf of Wall Street*.

The Wolf of Wall Street

Unstuck in time?

As Chicago Cubs fans used to say, anyone can have a bad century. Not so long ago, bankers and other finance professionals were in the midst of having a bad half-century, albeit bad only in the sense of its not being great. From the early

1930s, with its financial sector collapse, through the end of the 1970s, "banking was, well, boring" (Krugman 2009), offering wages that were merely comparable to those available elsewhere in the economy (Philippon and Reshef 2009, 3).

Far short though this fell of creating outright financial sector misery, its cultural impact, in a negative "dog that didn't bite" sense, was pervasive and unmistakable. Bankers and their ilk simply disappeared from books and films as commanding present-day figures for either good or ill. Thus, for nearly four decades, *It's a Wonderful Life* had no successor among prominent Hollywood releases in focusing on the derelictions of a rich banker.

During this time, one might see pointed Hollywood critiques of such mainstream institutions as the following: (1) big business (e.g., *The Godfather I and II*, 1972 and 1974) , (2) the mass media (e.g., *Face in the Crowd*, 1957, and *Network*, 1976), (3) advertising agencies (e.g., *Will Success Spoil Rock Hunter?*, 1957, and *Putney Swope*, 1969), and (4) office life (e.g., *The Man in the Grey Flannel Suit*, 1956, and *The Apartment*, 1960). There was not, however, a similar focus on banking or finance in particular, as it seemed not to need taking down.

Then, however, "[f]rom 1980 onwards, another dramatic shift occurred. The financial sector became a high-skill high-wage industry again" (Philippon and Reshef 2009, 8). Popular culture swiftly took notice. *Trading Places*, released in 1983, was the first prominent Hollywood commercial release since *It's a Wonderful Life* to feature powerful financial sector villains: a pair of overweening commodities brokers who callously play God with people's lives. Other entries in the antifinance genre soon followed. By the time of *Wall Street* (1987 film), *Bonfire of the Vanities* (1987 book and 1990 film), and *American Psycho* (1991 book and 2000 film), it had become clear that audiences would readily accept the premise that people in finance not only are important and powerful but might also be transgressive and dangerous.

Certain of these early entries also created new cultural tropes that have since proven enduring. *Bonfire of the Vanities* popularized the phrase "Masters of the Universe" to describe financiers' self-perceptions. *Wall Street* featured Gordon Gekko's "Greed is good!" speech, along with the revelation that he was using this rhetoric to rationalize cheating and would likely soon be going to prison. Over the course of time, innumerable real-world people, such as Martin Shkreli and the actual Jordan Belfort, raptly noted this meme's bad-boy glamor.

The 1980s also saw the rise of real-world financial sector scandals and controversy. Ivan Boesky, for example, had become a billionaire (in today's dollars) by 1986, when he appeared on the cover of the *Time* magazine. By the end of 1987, he had been sentenced to three years in jail. 1987 also featured a wrenching illustration of finance's renewed capacity to disrupt the real economy, what with the almost instantaneous 30 percent stock market decline that occurred on "Black Monday" (October 19, 1987), prompting fears of another Great Depression.

In the ensuing decades, finance-related scandals and economic disasters would just keep coming. The savings-and-loan crisis dated from the mid-1980s through the mid-1990s. The turn of the century brought multiple corporate governance scandals, featuring such now-infamous firms as Enron and WorldCom. This was followed, just a few years later, by the Great Recession of 2007–2009, brought on in large part by big Wall Street firms' reckless gambling and financial chicanery.

In *The Wolf of Wall Street*, we get the cultural residue of all these events blended together. The film follows Jordan Belfort's eponymous memoir in dramatizing the financial frauds that he and his colleagues at Stratton Oakmont had actually perpetrated from its foundation in 1989 through its shutdown by federal regulators in 1996. Even as a true(-ish) story, however, the memoir bears a broader pop-cultural stamp regarding Wall Street. Black Monday launched Belfort's career at Stratton Oakmont by getting him laid off at a traditional Wall Street firm. Moreover, he seems to have fully inhaled finance's rising black-hat cultural reputation. He mentions the "Masters of the Universe" meme right on page 1 (Belfort 2007, 1), and had headed to Wall Street in the first place because it was obviously the place to get rich fast.

By the time Belfort wrote this memoir, enough time had passed for Enron to join the list of familiar bywords for financial corruption. And by the time the film came out in 2013, the Great Recession had been added to the mix. All this seems to have helped make the film's depiction of finance a kind of cultural amalgam of all of the preceding decades' financial scandals.

Thus, consider the scene, not taken from the book, in which Jordan meets (and tries to bribe) FBI Agent Denham on his luxury yacht. Jordan's statement that Denham ought to look, not at Stratton Oakmont, but at the likes of "Goldman, Lehman Brothers, Merrill" anachronistically invokes our knowledge of how these firms had figured in Great Recession malfeasance. Back in the 1990s, where the scene is set, while they were already long famous, they had not yet acquired the scandalous notoriety that makes his reference to them seem so apt today.

So much for looking back. More spookily, *Wolf* also seems to look a few years forward and to anticipate the Trump era. While Jordan Belfort is almost a saint by Donald Trump standards—for example, he actually does sometimes care, at least modestly and ephemerally, about other people's feelings and welfare—his brashness, vulgarity, mendacity, cabal of worshippers, rhetoric of winners versus losers, and focus on success at all costs bring to mind the equally depraved, although far more malignant, monster who would soon place his fangs on America's throat.

Yin and yang

Just as George Bailey is a very 1930s figure, so the *Wolf* film's Jordan Belfort reeks of the more recent decades that gave us Enron, Bernie Madoff, and Trump. Jordan is fanatically devoted to getting rich. He despises the poor, and callously exploits them until realizing, to his initial surprise, that gullible rich people make even better targets. Meanwhile, he cheerily trumpets throughout his indifference or even hostility to conventional moral values.

Jordan would verge on being a figure out of Ayn Rand—his vulgarity, excess and avowed economic parasitism notwithstanding—if only he were far more bitter and insecure and had much less fun. However, rather than spew resentful, self-pitying venom like that of a John Galt, he spreads and lives by the gospel that "greed is fun" (Scott 2013). At least on the surface, he makes Stratton Oakmont a riotous "place of inclusion […] carnal excess," and "Rabelaisian laughter" (Burgoyne 2018, 51), as it operates in a "ludic, festive space of collective celebration" (Echart and Castrillo 2018, 61) and debauchery. Jordan is always selling his followers on the wealth/hedonistic pleasure nexus—no less relentlessly and self-interestedly than Trump would later rouse and delight his red-hatted audiences with the theme that hatred and cruelty are fun (Serwer 2018).

Jordan also champions perhaps the most fervidly optimistic version of the American Dream ever committed to film. If you want to get rich, he insists—and proves, by causing the "absolute morons" among his friends to be extravagantly compensated as his workplace lieutenants—you don't need any form of merit to succeed. Sheer desperation is enough. "I don't care if you graduated from Harvard or Buttfuck University or never got past fourth fucking grade!," he shouts to his brokers right before a Steve Madden initial public offering (IPO) earns the firm $22 million in just three hours. Nor need one have any skills, intelligence, knowledge, judgment, or taste. "That phone is the great equalizer!" All it takes is so to hate failure that "you'll have no choice but to do whatever it takes to win!"

Yet, even granting all the "fun," *Wolf* does little to support Jordan's belief in the "unshakable" pairing between wealth and happiness (Echart and Castrillo 2018, 61). He admits, for example, to feeling pervasive "anxiety" and "tension." While he says this in the course of apparently "hitting on" his wife's much older Aunt Emma—making it perhaps a strategic plea for help in releasing the "tension"—his behavior throughout confirms the self-diagnosis. Consider the following three signposts of his inner mental state:

(1) Jordan finds ordinary consciousness intolerable. This is a man who thoroughly accepts his first lesson in the stock-selling business (from Matthew McConaughey, in a hilarious cameo as Mark Hanna), to the effect that only massive quantities of cocaine, alcohol, and sexual gratification can possibly make psychologically tolerable the activity of "selling garbage" to anonymous "schmucks" on the phone. Much later, Jordan cannot bear the thought of having to sit through a flight from New York to Switzerland—even in first class, surrounded by a large, unruly contingent of his Stratton Oakmont minions—unless he can take enough Quaaludes to achieve oblivion.

(2) Conning and overawing the "schmucks," so that they will buy the "garbage" he has on offer, is so dire and adversarial a contest of wills as to require harnessing one's rage. Early on, Jordan amusingly acts out for his colleagues his contempt for, and hostility toward, a hapless pitch target whose voice he has placed on speaker. He later calls Stratton Oakmont's telephones "loaded M16[s]," and urges his brokers to "ram Steve Madden stock down your clients' throats and make them choke on it […]. Be telephone fucking terrorists!!"

(3) Jordan casually risks his life (and that of a copilot) by crash-landing a helicopter at 3:00 a.m. on the lawn of his Gatsbyesque Long Island mansion, while so overmedicated that he cannot see straight. This is partly bravado—a culturally familiar embrace of what I call "Hunter Thompson chic," which is itself sociologically revealing—but it also suggests a genuine death wish. In keeping with the credo of Hunter Thompson chic, Jordan takes great pride, not just in regularly getting "completely fucked-up" on drugs, but also in "gambl[ing] like a degenerate, drink[ing] like a fish, fuck[ing] hookers maybe five times a week, and hav[ing] three different Federal agencies looking to indict me." Whether he more deeply values transgression for its own sake, or willfully taking reckless risks just to show how audacious he is, remains unclear.

Also darkening the picture, Jordan's version of the American Dream is not just about hope and possibility. While touting upward mobility in the strongest terms possible, he depicts pursuing success as wholly predatory. Moreover, he views America's treatment of the rich, as opposed to the poor, in terms so starkly dichotomous that one might almost be in feudal France. The poor, in his view and experience, are pathetically deprived and face constant humiliation, while the rich get pleasure, privilege, and constant deference. Worse still, the very fact that anyone who tries hard enough should be able to get rich makes it all too clear that, if you fail, you must be a contemptible loser. This is not exactly a soothing message for those who are still seeking success in the ongoing struggle.

Wolf develops these darker angles, alongside Jordan's embrace of opportunity and "fun," by mirroring *Wonderful Life*'s internal ambiguity. Here, however, rather than deploying dueling narratives and counternarratives, *Wolf* has Jordan openly stating the "philosophical" premises behind everything he does, through voiceovers to us and speeches to his minions at Stratton Oakmont, only to have them undermined, both by so much else that we see in the film and by his own status as a charming yet repugnant antihero. The contrast gives us a yin and yang that have together perplexed and divided *Wolf*'s critics.

Rise of the antihero

In the famous Season 1 "College" episode of *The Sopranos*, Tony Soprano strangles a mobster-turned-snitch in the FBI witness protection program, whom he happens to spot while touring college campuses with his daughter. The episode aired despite the misgivings of HBO executives, who warned the showrunner: "You've created one of the most compelling characters in television in the last twenty years and you're going to ruin him in the fifth episode! […]. He kills that guy! We're going to lose the audience!" (Martin 2013, 92). They found out, of course, that viewers were quite willing to accept a dramatic lead who strangles someone with "unmitigated relish" (91), before going on to murder, both personally and by order, even close family members with whom both he and the audience have developed strong emotional bonds.

This rise of the antihero represents an important cultural change even from post–Hays Production Code Hollywood films like *The Godfather*. While Michael Corleone becomes a violent criminal who kills or destroys people whom both he and we care about, his reasons for adopting this path demand sympathy. Initially, he chooses law-abiding respectability instead of the family business. He changes course only when it becomes necessary to save his father's life, and then to punish the would-be killers. Thus, the reasons for his choice are no less commendable than those impelling, say, Telemachus in *The Odyssey* to join his father in slaughtering the suitors. Tony Soprano, by contrast, never in adulthood considers a different life, and his choice is, at best, somewhat excused by the early psychological wounds inflicted on him by a horrifying mother.

Michael even, at the end of *The Godfather, Part Two*, gets the proper sendoff for a flawed tragic hero, via his apparent sad realization that all his triumphs have somehow miscarried.[9] No such moment of insight comes for Tony, even if we deem it clear that *The Sopranos* ends with his murder.

Audiences' clearly demonstrated (by 2013) willingness to embrace charming sociopaths was clearly vital to both the creation and the public reception of *The Wolf of Wall Street*. It features, after all, a protagonist who makes money through fraud and deception, and asks rhetorically about one of his schemes: "[W]as it legal? Absolutely not. But we were making more money than we knew what to do with." He also cheats on both of his wives, egregiously mistreats women more generally, organizes offensive dwarf-tossing and head-shaving festivities at work, and boasts that, "on a daily basis, I take enough drugs to sedate Manhattan, Long Island, and Queens for a month."

Worse still, Jordan "never displays any remorse; there is no narrative comeuppance, no rebuke from anyone whose moral authority he recognizes" (Bradshaw 2014), and no hint of final punishment despite his being sent briefly to a country-club jail. As the film ends, a "rapt audience" that has paid amply for the privilege is sitting there agog, "eager to learn the techniques of persuasion that will part people from their money" (Murdock 2018, 37).

When an audience buys into enjoying the exploits of a charming but sociopathic fictional antihero, it may be hard to say what their stance toward him really is. They may not have settled on it themselves and, insofar as they have, it may vary with the individual and the instance. For example, if, despite the antihero's immorality, they are actively rooting for him as they watch, is this licensed by the fact that it is just fiction, and hence a safe realm for fantasy identification? Or would they also root for him in the real world, like so many Trump supporters showering unstinting loyalty on a transparently cruel, selfish, dishonest, ignorant, incompetent, delusional, and cowardly cartoon villain? Hence, for *The Wolf of Wall Street*, a much-asked question is how to read its attitude toward all the immorality, criminality, vulgarity, hyper-materialism, debauchery, and exploitation that Leonardo DiCaprio, as Jordan Belfort, so avidly and charismatically celebrates.

---

9 *The Godfather, Part 2*'s final scene shows Michael sitting alone on a lawn, after he has killed everyone left against whom he still held a grudge. A flashback shows him remembering a family gathering from December 1941 that is full of people who are all now either dead or estranged from him—both despite and, in some cases, because of his efforts. *The Godfather, Part 3*, if one chooses to heed its existence, then further shows Michael's feelings of penitence.

To some, *Wolf* is "not only [...] the most anti-Wall Street movie I've ever seen from a major director, but a scathing indictment of the American Dream, or what's become of it in an age of extreme inequality and decadent consumerism" (Rollert 2014). Its portraying "finance capital [as] itself [...] a form of high-level gangsterism" (Burnham 2016, 118) has been said to offer us a "libidinized version of Occupy Wall Street or Thomas Piketty's *Capital*" (131).

Others, however, note *Wolf*'s "outrageous delight" (Brody 2014) in Jordan's "essential vitality" (Brody 2013) and complain that we only see his perspective, not that of his victims (Wheat 2013). Still others rightly observe that *Wolf* simply refuses to choose between "offer[ing] a sustained and compelling diagnosis of the terminal pathology that afflicts us" and being an "especially florid symptom of the disease" (Haas 2015, 260).

In this debate, both sides are right, except insofar as each deems the other to be wrong. The seductiveness, not just of Jordan Belfort himself, but of what he stands for, is an important part of the takeaway—whether or not one is oneself partly seduced, in addition to being appalled. Either way, however, Jordan is both plausible and grotesque whenever he steps out of mere dialogue with other characters to express his "philosophy" directly, often with deliberately outrageous overstatement, through his voiceovers and speeches. Indeed, he does this with sufficient frequency to provide a useful set of core assertions that the film both supports and refutes.

View of the rich

The gospel according to Jordan Belfort has three main elements that relate to wealth and the rich. First, he defines class purely monetarily, rather than in terms of any noncash social markers, such as birth, manners, morals, or education. Second, he provides an account of how, in keeping with the American Dream, those who deserve success can find it, no matter where they started out. Third, he explains why becoming rich is so compellingly important. In each case, some of what he says is either contradicted by what we see, incompletely convincing even to him, or rooted in an underlying desperation and neediness that undermine, even as they evidently motivate, his smooth salesmanship.

Defining class purely monetarily

Less than a minute into the film, when Jordan first breaks the fourth wall by using voiceover to address the film audience, he says: "I am a former member of the middle class raised by two accountants in a tiny apartment in Bayside, Queens."

There is a pause, then he adds: "The year I turned 26, I made 49 million dollars as the head of my own brokerage firm"—followed by another pause—"which really pissed me off because it was three shy of a million a week."

The rimshot comedy timing alerts us, if we have not already caught on, to the film's frenziedly comic and satiric tone—within Scorsese's oeuvre, echoing not just *Goodfellas* (Orr 2013) but also such cringe-farces as *The King of Comedy* and *After Hours*. Beyond that, however, we here first encounter Jordan's insistence, perhaps a bit more vehement than it needs to be, that class is purely a matter of how much money one has.

Both here and elsewhere in *Wolf*, Jordan resolutely proclaims the "existence of a new form of social aristocracy. To be part of the privileged class—to be among the best—no longer depends on one's knowledge, virtue, social skills, or family name, but rather, it hinges on the ability to amass exorbitant amounts of money (which are earned, needless to say, by reaching into others' pockets). It is, therefore, a monetary aristocracy" (Echart and Castrillo 2018, 63).

Yet we see plenty of evidence in tension with this view, even as an account of Jordan's beliefs. Traditional markers and attributes of class affect perceptions and behavior in ways that at least modify the ostensibly stand-alone importance of money that he so eagerly proclaims.

Indeed, even in the film's first minute, before we hear his pronouncement that he has definitively left behind his middle-class origins, we observe the optical importance of pedigree. *Wolf* opens by showing us a pompous commercial for Stratton Oakmont, which is portrayed (in Jordan's later words) as "patrician and blue-blooded," not to mention sleekly yuppie, rather than in keeping with its actual raucous and seedy character. This suggests the continued importance of appearing to be traditionally upper class—as seemingly should not be necessary if aristocracy has become a purely monetary concept.

The incentive to deploy a genteel outer layer might not significantly modify the monetary character of Jordan's vision of aristocracy if that layer could, with sufficient ease, be purchased or simulated by anyone with sufficient cash. In this regard, consider his dubbing his soon-to-be second wife Naomi the "Duchess of Bay Ridge." This combines treating noble-sounding titles as if they still mattered apart from just money, with allowing them to be granted at will, at least by him. Moreover, her being the proposed Duchess of so blue-collar a place as Bay Ridge—*Wolf* is highly cognizant of the status gap between Manhattan and the outer boroughs—gives the title an almost mocking sound, although the mockery's main direction—at traditional Duchesses, or at her?—is ambiguous. Thus, his giving her this monicker could equally be seen as contradicting, or else confirming, aristocracy's now purely monetary character.

In other respects, however, *Wolf* clearly shows that traditional class concepts and manners remain important. For example:

- Jordan is uncomfortable with, and even intimidated by, people with truly upper-class social credentials. The two such people whom we meet in *Wolf* are Jean-Jacques Saurel, the Swiss banker, and Naomi's Aunt Emma (Burnham 2016, 122). Jordan and Saurel hate each other on sight, a response triggered by Saurel's distaste for Jordan's lack of manners. Meanwhile, Jordan is uncharacteristically impressed, but also made uneasy, by Aunt Emma, who finds him delectably amusing.
- Jordan periodically expresses resentment of "Harvard" types, whom he exhorts the Stratton Oakmont sales force to outperform. Populist resentment also features in a scene in which Donnie Azoff, his second-in-command, excites the troops before the Madden IPO by humiliating and firing a bow-tied Stratton broker with a goldfish. Traditional class markers would not be worth thus desecrating if they did not still retain some prestige.
- Jordan contributes to his own downfall through a parvenu's lack of grounding in elite behavioral norms. For example, his crude efforts (against the advice of counsel) to charm, bribe, or intimidate Agent Denham show a counterproductive naïveté. People who work at the firms that he tells Denham "you *should* be looking at" in lieu of Stratton—Goldman, Lehman Brothers, and Merrill—not only are less "unorthodox," as he puts it, but also are more attuned to decorous social norms that help to preserve regulatory tolerance for their own undoubted wrongdoing.

Despite all this, one should not exaggerate the degree to which Jordan seems driven by resentment of the better-born. He is too self-focused for that. Instead, the mania that we will see pervades his "philosophical" premises, no less than his behavior, seems far more rooted in the downward-looking need to distinguish oneself from the herd than in any such upward-looking animus. This, in turn, reflects the American Dream's clear message (at least, as he interprets it) that, if you have the chance to succeed and yet do not, you must be a pathetic and contemptible loser.

The road to riches

As a fervid champion of the American Dream's realism and attainability, Jordan cannot easily be outdone, even by the likes of a Russell Conwell or a John Galt if one gives an American cast to his rants about how genius inevitably triumphs whether one was poor or rich to start. Yet Jordan also could hardly differ more from those two with regard to just how he sees one achieving success. Again, Conwell grounds success in knowing people well enough to understand what they want, while Galt credits it to a mighty intellect's jousting with the Universe until it yields its secrets.

For Jordan, by contrast, the path to success is unabashedly predatory. Consider "Sell me this pen," the training exercise he uses both with his Stratton protégés and in the motivational success lectures he is offering at the film's end. The object to be sold is chosen simply because it is trivial and on hand, and hence useful for proving that one can "sell anything." The aim is to create bogus demand for it.

The best answer Jordan ever gets to this challenge is from Brad, his drug dealer friend who is doing too well to join Stratton as an executive. "Could you do me a favor?," Brad asks Jordan in the role play. "Write down your name on a napkin for me."—"I don't have a pen."—"Exactly. Supply and demand, my friend." In short, one simply and manipulatively creates the demand that one then conveniently satisfies.

Jordan furthers his protégés' education in salesmanship by explaining that phone marketing is purely a contest of wills. "Whoever speaks first, loses." The emollient, of course, is shameless lying, as epitomized by his first sale, when he starts at the Investor's Center, of a stock called Aerotyne that is currently selling for 6 cents a share.

In truth, Aerotyne amounts to some "guys [...] [who] make radar detectors out of a garage in Dubuque." On the phone, however, it becomes "an extremely exciting investment opportunity [that] crossed my desk today," and ostensibly one of only five per year that his firm will recommend. Aerotyne features in his spiel as a "cutting edge tech firm out of the Midwest, awaiting imminent patent approval on a new generation of radar equipment." Jordan notes the true arithmetical fact that, if the stock price were to rise from 6 cents to a dollar, then a $3,000 investment would appreciate to $50,000, before closing with the lie that his firm's (nonexistent) "research indicates" that it could actually go "much, much higher." This performance, of course, elicits slack-jawed admiration from all the others in the Investor's Center's boiler room.

Jordan could not be more clear-eyed about the lack of any true wealth creation or societal enrichment from what he does. As Mark Hanna says about stock-selling early on: "We don't create shit; we don't build anything." In similar spirit, Jordan later avers to Agent Denham that, in "the world we live in, the jobs with real value, the ones we should appreciate—firefighters, teachers, FBI agents—those are the ones we pay the least."

If getting rich is purely predatory and zero-sum—as in a Donald Trump view of "deals," in which there is a winner and a loser, rather than any possibility of mutual advantage—then how can allowing great wealth accumulation be rationalized? Jordan's answer, it appears, is one part cynical—that is simply the way things are—and one part character test. If absolutely everyone wants to get rich, as Jordan insists to his protégés (unmoved by the posited counterexamples of Amish furniture makers and Buddhists), then economic competition is simply nature's way of allocating the prizes, and who are we to question it? Jordan might make a good Social Darwinist, if only he read more and cared more. But he would be one without any belief that the elemental struggle fuels societal progress.

Why is it good to be rich?

Why does Jordan value getting rich? This might seem to be the proverbial fake "trick question"—one that not only appears to be completely obvious, but in fact is. Yet the question is indeed more complicated than it might initially seem. Jordan's thirst for wealth, rather than being primarily about the joys of avid material consumption, is more responsive to concerns about relative status.

Jordan is, after all, a person who says about his second wife: "The day I met Naomi was the day I truly became the Wolf. Every guy wanted her—so I *had* to have her." The point is less her sexual allure than forcing other people to envy him.

In similar vein, he explains in voiceover that "[m]oney doesn't just buy you a better life—better food, better cars, better pussy—it also makes you a better person. You can give generously to the church of your choice or the political party. You can save the fucking spotted owl with money."

Later he says, in a speech to the Strattonites just before the Madden IPO: "There is no nobility in poverty. I've been rich, and I've been poor, and I choose rich every time. At least as a rich man, when I have to face my problems, I show up in the back of a limo wearing a $2,000 suit and $40,000 gold watch!" When he says this, he already knows that the "problems" he will soon be facing include the substantial threat of prosecution and jail.

In each of these instances, the point is to be better-off than other people, whose inferiority to oneself gives pleasure. However, Jordan is also, more pragmatically, mindful of power, extracting deference, and being treated well by others with power. "It's amazing the kind of loyalty money will buy," he says, when his friends and the police almost kill his butler on suspicion of stealing from him. Later on, when Jordan fears prison before realizing that (of course) he will be sent to a country club version with outdoor tennis courts, he says: "For a brief, fleeting moment I'd forgotten I was rich and lived in America."

In sum, on the front end, Jordan's America remains the land of opportunity—albeit one in which the battle for success is purely predatory and manipulative. On the back end, however, it mocks any notion that egalitarianism, democracy, or the neutral provision of justice might retain any of their long-celebrated sway. This vision of predatory plutocracy gets etched in all the more firmly when we turn to Jordan's view of the poor.

View of the poor

In his pre–Madden IPO speech to the Strattonites, Jordan follows up his reference to the comfort of facing problems with a $40,000 gold watch by visualizing the poor loser who should choose to

> depart this room full of winners [...]. [O]ne day in the not-so-distant future, you'll be sitting at a red light in your beat-up old Pinto, and [a winner who stayed at Stratton is] gonna pull up in a brand new Porsche, with their gorgeous young wife at their side. And who will you be next to? Some ugly beast with three days of razor-stubble in a sleeveless moo-moo, crammed in next to you with a carload of groceries from the fucking Price Club!

(Nearly all of the Strattonites in the audience are men, and anyone, such as Donnie, who is not exclusively heterosexual is presumably trying to pass.)

Once again, this is only superficially about better versus worse cars, or about women as lust objects being evaluated based on their physical appeal to heterosexual man-boys. It also is about more than just relative status, strongly though Jordan emphasizes this aspect by having the "winner" and "loser" stare at each other while at a red light that is the only place their paths would ever cross. Beyond all that, Jordan emphasizes the utter, abject shame that one faces if one has become the man in the Pinto. There is no happiness, no dignity, and nothing to feel good about once one has been exposed as a loser. One's own belief system commands despising oneself.

As American as apple pie, these sentiments richly fulfill the logic behind the American Dream, once one has stripped away any notion (which was always psychologically secondary—a convenient rationalization) that wealth-seeking might serve any broader social purposes, such as satisfying authentic consumer demand or enabling economic progress. The quest for wealth becomes a test just for the sake of having a test, identifying winners because that is what we care about and because no human qualities matter other than winning. Kindness, generosity, taste, manners, wit, wisdom, knowledge, understanding: these and any other such non-monetary qualities are all just nothings. They are perhaps pathetically to be invoked by losers, who cannot otherwise even try to counter their own well-earned despondency, but winners don't need them, and such qualities don't really matter to anyone anyway.

Suppose Jordan secretly doubts that this all-American vision is entirely true. Then he might be embracing it all the more fiercely because (once he has become rich) it quiets criticism of his personal worthiness from any more humanistic perspective. If he feels any such doubts, however, they are well concealed. Moreover, his vision of the success credo is already dystopian enough to produce the substantial distress that we otherwise see him trying to allay, without one's needing to posit that he finds it facially unpersuasive.

Private morals and social morality

As we saw earlier, *It's a Wonderful Life* suggests the importance of conventional morality—both altruistic and viciously self-denying—in keeping the ambitious and gifted attuned to social justice, rather than just to their own self-fulfillment. *Wonderful Life* thereby invites one to forecast, as *The Wolf of Wall Street* indeed confirms, that compassion and empathy will perish in the steam explosion if ever the valves cease to hold. *Wolf* also, however, rebuts thinking that, without the pressure valves, at least the newly minted sociopaths might find contentment and happiness. Instead, the American Dream now reaches a newly unsettling level of urgency, reflecting the parched psychic landscape in which "winning" is the only thing.

One sign of Jordan's distress is his embrace of Hunter Thompson chic, denoting a credo of insouciant risk-taking in the service of a quest for oblivion. A second is his eagerness to view Stratton Oakmont as a benign and supportive office family—a haven from the war of all against all, in which hilarity and shared excess lubricate the full collective embrace of an internally benign communal spirit. The first of these psychic responses to the stressfulness of winner takes all is merely pathetic. The second is thoroughly debunked by much of what we see in the film.

Hunter Thompson chic

When Jordan boasts that he daily "take[s] enough drugs to sedate Manhattan, Long Island, and Queens for a month"—and, along with the usual list of associated vices, even has "three different Federal agencies looking to indict me"—the cultural part that he is playing dates back many decades. Hunter Thompson injected it into the modern American cultural mainstream in works such as *Fear and Loathing in Las Vegas* (1971), with its famous opening line: "We were somewhere around Barstow on the edge of the desert when the drugs began to take hold."

Thompson portrays himself as wildly out of control, taking crazy risks as he pharmaceutically self-induces hallucination, mania, slobbering, ecstasy, and paranoia, mostly in front of uncomprehending squares who range from the contestants in a dirt-biking race to corporate hospitality specialists, to drug enforcement police. Millions have read his work with delight, while millions more have absorbed his image of the proudly drug-addled outlaw, even if only through such watered-down tributes as Uncle Duke in *Doonesbury* or the beer-swigging "wild and crazy guys" from late-1970s *Saturday Night Live* skits. Thompson's drug-crazed outlaw has remained a potent American cultural image ever since, especially among young males, denoting relatable outrageousness and outsiderism.

As Hampton Stevens (2011) notes, "[t]he depth to which Thompson's sensibility and persona has permeated American mass consciousness is simply staggering." Hence, Jordan's appropriation of such an image, while he is also playing the roles of well-scrubbed salesman, charismatic self-help preacher, self-styled "Bond villain," and ersatz Gatsby, should come as no surprise. Seemingly mixing impulse with calculation, its implications include:

- Situating him as a rebel and nonconformist, at odds with what one might expect from the head of a financial firm worth hundreds of millions of dollars.
- Establishing him as cool, fearless, and fun-loving. The zhlubs who admire and laugh with a Hunter Thompson or a Jordan Belfort know full well that they would never dare to, or be able to, live their own lives so audaciously.
- Suggesting a self-destructiveness that hints at self-hatred. The late-night helicopter landing is only one of the occasions on which Jordan risks his life, his health, or his freedom, often for little evident reason.

Like any so massively successful a cultural meme, Hunter Thompson chic has flexible and varying grounds for appeal. To people who are living dull and constricted lives, or who are being forced toward conventional (even if materially rewarding) paths, it offers heady, liberating escapism. This seems less applicable, however, to a high achiever like Jordan, who not only makes a huge fortune but also gets to set his own rules while playing the Pied Piper to what Forbes Magazine calls his "merry band of brokers." It is partly, of course, a schtick that he deliberately uses to become their supposed Robin Hood. Yet it also shows signs of expressing the agony and jaded emptiness that he finds in a self-created (but very American) world of cutthroat struggle for high stakes, set against a cultural wasteland where there is nothing to value or enjoy apart from material success.

Stratton Oakmont as "America," family, and sanctuary

Lest one think that Jordan has no ideals whatsoever, consider the following words from a speech to the Strattonites:

> [T]he very idea of Stratton is that when you come here and step into this bullpen for the first time, you start your life anew. You have a place here and no one can take that away from you! Stratton Oakmont is America! Give me your tired and poor! The very moment you walk through that door and pledge your loyalty to this firm, you become part of a family, you become a Strattonite!

In short, tribal loyalty means everything that all the other social and ethical bonds we might ever encounter in *Wolf* do not. All for one, apparently, and one for all. This ideal, if taken at face value, would make Stratton Oakmont a unique haven from a cold-blooded world in which people are generally only marks to be exploited, sex objects to be used, rivals to be disparaged and impressed, or else beneath notice.

Jordan gives this speech when he is planning to step down as CEO and make a lenient settlement with the U.S. Securities and Exchange Commission (SEC), thereby derailing the FBI probe, and allowing him to "[s]ail into the sunset" still a multimillionaire. We get proof that he actually believes what he is saying, at least right as he stands there, because, relishing the adulation, he actually talks himself into rejecting the SEC deal and staying at Stratton. This verges on being a calamitous mistake—albeit made far less dire by America's coddling of rich white-collar criminals, along with Jordan's ability to make a new fortune as a motivational speaker, after his release from jail.

One should not, however, too fully credit his idealization of the Stratton workplace, given other things that we see. It is a place, for example, where a female sales assistant is paid $10,000 to have her head shaved in front of a jeering male audience. Jordan explains that "she's using the money for

breast implants! Is this a great company or what?!!" But even if one were
to overlook the ugly sexism—at a firm where women, both employees and
the constant stream of visiting prostitutes, are continually being degraded—
the young woman's look of terror as she is being shaved supports a less
benign narrative. And lest we think that only women are mistreated at
Stratton, recall the scene with the bow-tied broker and his goldfish, or how
Steve Madden is heckled, and pelted with his own designer shoes, when
Jordan pushes him out front just before the IPO.

Stratton is a drunken, rape-culture-steeped, gay-bashing frat house, with
enough Lord of the Flies elements—and, one presumes, job performance
pressures—to lay anxiety on even the most privileged young heterosexual White
males who might work there. Indeed, Jordan tells us as much:

> In order to keep these guys working, I gotta keep 'em spending. I need to
> keep them chasing the dream […]. I could afford to pay them more, but then
> they wouldn't need me as much. And as long as they need me they'll always
> fear me.

We also learn just how deep loyalty runs at Stratton Oakmont when Jordan
agrees to be a "rat," wear a wire, and deliver his associates to the feds. He initially
tips off Donnie with a warning note about the wire, but Donnie's way of
repaying the favor is to hand the note to the authorities. Jordan then responds
by "g[i]v[ing] up everyone," to the extent of aiding two dozen convictions and
earning a substantially reduced sentence.

The bonfire of the American Dream

The Wolf of Wall Street is but one of the many finance movies since the 1980s
to emphasize fraud, the culture of greed, the abuse of customer and client
relationships, and the toxicity of the "boiler room." Nor is it unique in focusing
on an ambitious, upwardly mobile young man—albeit one who, unlike Charlie
Sheen's Bud Fox in *Wall Street*, seems to need only Mark Hanna's few minutes
of mentoring to emerge, fully formed, from the chrysalis. Its depicting extreme
lewdness and depravity reflects not only a shrewd commercial instinct but also
Stratton Oakmont's fringe character among finance firms.

Within this crop, however, *Wolf* stands out as unusually, not just entertaining
(if queasy-making) but forthright and insightful in linking the late twentieth-
century re-rise of finance to comorbidities within American popular culture.
This is no mere bonfire of the vanities, but of the American Dream.

Merely wanting to succeed and rise, and believing that one can, is a large part of what made America appealing to millions of people around the world for so many decades, and indeed centuries, perhaps still continuing today. But when an ostensibly featureless social landscape—and worse still, one haunted by racism and White supremacy—makes wealth the supreme test, not just of how well you will live, but of whether you have any value as a human being, there is a risk of outsized dysfunction. Strains in the fabric like those presented by the re-rise of finance, and with it of extreme high-end inequality, can lead to a rupturing of ordinary decency and social connectedness. So, while *The Wolf of Wall Street* does not "predict" anything, it seems of a piece with such subsequent social developments as the rise of Trumpism, and the angry rejection by millions of any notion that they should treat, say, the rise of COVID-19 as calling for solidarity or responsible behavior toward others.

Summary: Living with the American Dream

Both *It's a Wonderful Life* and *The Wolf of Wall Street* feature a young man, born into the middle class, who is eager to rise economically and who exhibits social attitudes that reflect his own era. Thus, while neither George nor Jordan much likes or admires those who were born rich, only George feels a call to resist them. And while neither especially respects the poor, only George feels a moral obligation to help them, and only Jordan wholly embraces scorn and contempt for them.

The films are more parallel, however, in illustrating the American Dream's dual character as a judgment, not just a promise. It thereby contributes to the psychic pressures that lead George to the bridge, and Jordan to his rampant criminality and drug mania. Its drawing an implicit contrast between the mediocre many who fail, and the extraordinary few who succeed, also helps to fuel the downward hostility that we see in both films: by George toward the hapless many for whom he has had to sacrifice his own hopes, and by Jordan toward all the "schmucks" whose timid vacillation he and his henchmen must overpower on the phone.

American individualism does not have to imply sociopathy. But these two films—and *The Wolf of Wall Street* especially, from its vantage point astride the Second Gilded Age—help to show why it can, and indeed why, especially in ages of rampant high-end inequality, it so often does.

CHAPTER 5

CONCLUSION

Every act of writing about the past involves at least "implicitly chronicling [...] [one's] own times" (Snell 2015). In this book's focus on the past, however, the present is more than just implicit. A main impetus for my examining episodes from America's cultural and ideological past is the hope of shedding light on how and why we have gotten to our present state—one in which a slide to autocracy gravely threatens, and in which "national cohesion, voluntary sacrifice for the common good, and trust in institutions and each other" have declined so steeply as to compromise our effectually fighting a deadly pandemic (Brooks 2021). Both the evil forces that threaten us still and the anger radiating from all sides—in a country where, at least on the surface, a "cult of consensus" (Higham 1959) prevailed not all that long ago—prompt asking what durable American attributes might lie behind both types of periods (but especially ours).

Across multiple eras, little has been more American than debating what it means to be *un*-American. President Biden recently used the term to describe antidemocratic voting restrictions. Yet, as a matter of history, they are evidently all too American. Correct usage turns on whether one defines "American" in terms of our ideals or our practices. Depending on this terminological choice, nothing could be more un-American, or alternatively more American, than the violent thuggery of the Ku Klux Klan and the January 6, 2021 insurrectionists.

For an earlier such terminological debate, albeit pitting ideals against ideals, rather than against practices, consider the era of McCarthyism. The infamous House Un-American Activities Committee expressly defined its quarry (who were presumed to support Soviet totalitarianism) as un-American. To Harry Truman, however, the Committee's efforts to punish dissent and enforce ideological conformity made *it* "the most un-American thing in the country today." In short, the adversaries in this debate, no less than America and England according to George Bernard Shaw, found themselves divided by a common language.

Tensions between American ideals and practices, and between rival American ideals, go all the way back to the founding. Only in America could so stirring a call for liberty and equality as the Declaration of Independence have been penned primarily by Thomas Jefferson, a slaveholder. Samuel Johnson's famous question, "How is it that we hear the loudest yelps for liberty among the drivers of Negroes?," could just as well have been a puzzled query, as a gibe.

More recently, Ayn Rand (1974) was playing a very old game when she lauded America as "the greatest, the noblest and, in its original founding principles, the *only* moral country in the history of the world"—based, however, on her audaciously rewriting history. Rather than acknowledging the indisputable fact that the values of both liberty *and* equality have deep historical roots here, she redefined the latter sentiment—rebranded as "mawkish concern with and compassion for the feeble, the flawed, the suffering, the guilty"—as not just un-American (that would never be enough for her) but rooted in "hatred for America."

Between them, Jefferson and Rand illustrate two key sources of tension and conflict that are embedded in American identity. The one is White supremacy's uneasy coexistence with our more high-flown ideals. The other is the difficulty of reconciling egalitarianism with market meritocracy, when the latter so strongly teaches that people are *not* equal. This book's emphasizing the conflicts around market meritocracy, far more than those around race, in no way contradicts recognizing their *mutual* importance. It leaves, however, room for the further question of how the two might interact with each other.

Market Meritocracy versus Egalitarianism

In Russell Conwell's Acres of Diamonds lecture from the First Gilded Age, the tension between core American values shows up in his predilection for couching his claims, on behalf of the superrich, in such overheated terms. Rather than just calling their fortunes well deserved, he insists that they are affirmatively better people than the rest of us: more honest, more caring, and more observant. And, lest anyone question the almost perfect overlap he claims between wealth and moral desert by pointing to fortunes that are merely inherited, rather than personally earned, he insists that "not one rich man's son out of seventeen ever dies rich." Inheriting wealth, he claims, is not just useless but a catastrophe—a point that he drives home with homophobic slurs regarding the heirs' supposed effeminacy.

Conwell also, more kindly and inclusively, insists that wisdom and salvation (along with riches) remain in reach for everyone. His view of

America as socially and economically permeable, with democratic manners prevailing throughout, may reflect how early he first wrote it—as I have said elsewhere, well before "the full flowering of the [Gilded Age's] social and economic transformations [...] [and] in a society with smaller and more permeable vertical gulfs than those that would open up" by the late nineteenth century (Shaviro 2020, 139, 159). Plausible description then turned to convenient archaism as the society evolved, while Conwell kept the lecture sufficiently current by adding denunciations of labor unions and left-wing orators.

Even with this darker turn, however, Conwell little prepares one for the bloodthirsty hysteria of Ayn Rand's verbal assaults on egalitarianism and democracy. If Rand's venom toward plebeians on behalf of the privileged had not so rapidly attracted an American mass audience that has lasted for decades, one might have thought it merely a florid case of narcissistic personality disorder, perhaps also reflecting her non-U.S. origins. Instead, however, both Randism's longstanding cultural resonance in the United States and the extent to which it anticipated Trumpism suggest that Rand had somehow discerned something fundamental about the tension in American culture between its core egalitarian and market meritocratic values.

Only in America could freedom so often feel like slavery in the overheated minds of her fanboys among "wealthy bankers, CEOs, tech moguls, and right-wing politicians" (Duggan 2019, 78), along with those merely hopeful of joining their ranks. Expressing boundless self-pity mixed with fragile self-confidence, Randites detect an unbearable insult in being asked to offer a modicum of respect to those who are (in reality or fantasy) less fortunate than themselves. Even the financial cost of being required to help fund a modest social safety net seems to matter less than the lack of genuflection that it evinces. While such rabid status anxiety is easier to detect than to explain, it may have as much to do with the fear that one is in truth a "loser," in a society where market success is so sacralized, as with that of being a "winner" who faces the threat of insolence from the "losers."

By the onset of the Trump era, Rand's "dour visage" could actually be said to "preside[] over the spirit of our times" (Duggan 2019, xi). Perhaps her cult is at last receding, or at least mutating as hatred for intellectuals (for her, merely a Lead Supporting Villain as compared to ordinary folk) overtakes, if not *all* hatred of the poor, then at least all such nonracist hatred. Still, Randism's rise from fringe cult to the informal bible of a mass movement stands as a continued warning that the marriage between America's egalitarianism and market meritocracy might catastrophically fail.

When we turn to *The Great Gatsby*, one of the most obvious changes from the Conwell and Galt lectures lies in the author's political viewpoint. Fitzgerald was on the left rather than the right politically, and sometimes called himself a socialist. He wrote with the aim of illustrating his conviction that "the very rich [...] are different from you and me," in ways didactically illustrated by his hostile depiction of the Buchanans. He also evinced enough skepticism toward what came to be known as the American Dream to support the conviction among 1950s literary critics that *Gatsby* had exposed it as "little more than a thinly veiled nightmare" (Bicknell 1954, 556).

Questions of political orientation aside, however, *Gatsby* gains considerable sociological interest from its being a work of fiction rather than a lecture and one written by an author who valued the aesthetic appeal of ambiguity and ambivalence. Thus, it frequently escapes from and even undermines its own apparent ideological schema. For example, consider its apparent proposition that people like the Buchanans, born to great wealth and from established families, stand alone at the undisputed top of the social pyramid. This gets undercut by the portrayal, at a Gatsby party, of "interesting people [...] who do interesting things"—movie stars and other such popular celebrities—whom we see drawing greater envy and social anxiety from Tom than he seems likely to draw from them.

Meanwhile, *Gatsby*'s ambivalence about rich people, whom it views not just as odious but also as fascinating, and its ambiguity regarding what we should make of its lead character's rise and fall have allowed it to function as a kind of Rorschach test for readers across the decades. It offers both catnip for the decorously discontented and vivid nose-against-the-glass voyeurism for the not so hopeful.

Given the book's apparent criticism of American culture (even if the criticism's grounds are somewhat opaque), its 1950s canonization may bespeak an era of greater national self-confidence than we have today—or, at least, one of less pervasive politicization of the culture wars. Not to worry, however: school boards' purging of *The Great Gatsby* from curricular reading lists, on the ground that it is too "controversial" (Taylor 2020), have already begun.

It's a Wonderful Life and *The Wolf of Wall Street* have enough in common for their differences to help illuminate some of the ways in which American attitudes toward the rich and the poor have changed between the Great Depression and today. In *It's a Wonderful Life*, George Bailey, if only he let himself, could almost compete with an Ayn Rand character in resenting and blaming the common folk whom he instead spends his life championing. Or, if he listened to the inner voice that he mostly suppresses, he could compete with Jordan Belfort in despising them. Yet old-fashioned moral strictures, aided by downward-looking empathy and communalism, along with upward-looking disgust and contempt, keep him grimly fixed on the path of the Progressive Hero and People's Champion, however ungratifying he may find this role.

Jordan Belfort, appropriately for the time when he started out, takes his own youthful hunger for importance and achievement straight into Wall Street finance. Once fully molted, he becomes a strikingly Trump-like figure, albeit minus the malignant firehose of ever-spewing rage and hatred. His drive to be an apex predator, and therefore a "winner" in a sea full of "losers," reflects the anxiety that comes from viewing economic outcomes as the sole and pitiless test of human worth. Even his most frenzied pleasure seeking yields little joy and no satisfaction, in a desolately philistine landscape where nothing matters but the muscle-flexing power of money. Given his drives and values, only by achieving great wealth can he sustain self-respect, and even that cannot quell his abiding boredom. Jordan's twisted Horatio Alger story, far more caustically than anything about the rise and fall of Jay Gatsby, portrays the American Dream as having become the posited "nightmare."

Adding in White Supremacy versus Egalitarianism

Long before the Revolution, the society that English immigrants had founded in North America was relying extensively on both genocide against Native Americans, and the mass enslavement of Black people. These practices' self-evidently poor fit with the Declaration of Independence's encomia to liberty and equality did not prevent the Declaration from decrying the British Crown's supposed incitement of "merciless Indian savages" and "domestic [slave] insurrections." Over time, however, the contradiction between stated values and observed practices grew harder to ignore.

Moreover, while the very success of the genocide against Native Americans allowed its prominence to decline, slavery's demise did not similarly push racial subordination offstage. Its replacement by a racially based caste system, paralleling India's centuries-long subordination of Dalit "untouchables" (Wilkerson 2020), ensured that the affront to liberty and (especially) equality would remain highly visible.

The mid-twentieth century dismantlement of formal racial discrimination dealt White supremacy a blow but did not conclusively defeat it. Forces seeking its retention or even expansion have remained active and vehement. They received an enormous shot of adrenaline, as yet unabated, when America in 2008 inflicted an apparently grievous dignitary wound on status-insecure White racists by electing Barack Obama (by their lights, a hurtfully poised Black man) as president. The rise of Birtherism and Trumpism promptly followed.

The battles pitting egalitarianism against market meritocracy on the one hand, and against white supremacy on the other, inevitably bear on each other. They are each too large, as well as too overlapping in their terrains, to have operated entirely separately. For example, returning to Samuel Johnson's question, could a slaveholding Jefferson's "yelping" for liberty really have just been fortuitous self-contradiction? The hypocrisy is too evident for it to have occurred only to outside observers.

Jefferson was, after all, a man who financed his own lavish personal spending by "pioneer[ing] the monetizing of slaves" (Wiencek 2012) and selling them as needed to secure ready cash. He was thus, in effect, selling enslaved persons to fund (among other things) his frequent and costly purchases of the latest European philosophical texts concerning liberty and justice. This is not to say, however, that his political and philosophical stance was *just* hypocrisy. It may also have emerged organically from the complex relationships between his multiple social roles and self-conceptualizations.

Thus, consider Jefferson's evident embarrassment about slavery, which he frequently criticized. This feeling may have reflected, not just its barbarity but also its association with Virginia's relatively backwoods and backward society, as compared to that of a more "civilized" England or France. Perhaps this unflattering contrast added to the appeal, both for Jefferson and many of his peers, of donning the cloak of the passionate Defender of Liberty. At the same time, however, the degradations that he saw being inflicted, and indeed was personally inflicting, on enslaved persons may have nourished in him a genuine horror regarding the threat of his own group's ever being subordinated by anyone. After all, he knew all too well what subordination could look like.

Turning to the works that I discuss in this book, neither Conwell nor the Galt speech discusses race. Ayn Rand, however, subsequently wrote (in 1963) an essay denouncing racism as "the lowest, most crudely primitive form of collectivism [...] [because it] ascrib[es] moral, social or political significance to a man's genetic lineage [...]. [Accordingly, t]he policy of the Southern states toward Negroes was and is a shameful contradiction of this country's basic principles." Yet she also voiced equal objection to the federal government's response to racism through "encroachment upon the legitimate rights of the states," and to "the new demands of the Negro leaders" for affirmative action racial quotas.

Rand also let the veil slip a bit in a 1974 speech to West Point military graduates. Here she defended the White settlers' centuries-long assault on

Native Americans by stating that "[a]ny white person who brings the elements of civilization had the right to take over this continent" (Norton 2015). She also, in this speech, mocked "people who claim that financial priority should be given to [...] classes in esthetic self-expression for the residents of the slums" (Rand 1974), thus showing her command of racist code words.

Even if one nonetheless were to declare Rand personally free of racism, her frequent political and cultural appeal to racists would come as no coincidence or surprise. At a minimum, it reflects the fact that "liberty" (for oneself especially) is easier than "equality" to square with the defense of racial subordination. Additionally, however, its roots in status anxiety fit well with the racist impulse to preserve Black subordination.

The Great Gatsby, unlike the other works discussed in this book, overtly addresses the American relationship between race and class. In it, we can see that Tom's too-vehement racism is déclassé and may say more about his own frustrations and sense of postcollegiate personal decline than about the supposed fate of civilization. We also, however, are treated by Fitzgerald to the cringeworthy "comedy" of the "modish Negroes" with their fancy limousine and white chauffeur, who purport to outshine Gatsby in his own too-garish "circus wagon." Then there is the stereotyped anti-Semitism of Wolfsheim's portrayal, enhanced by the repulsiveness of his hairy nostrils and human molar cufflinks.

Perhaps most telling with regard to race and class, however, is the book's suggestion that Jimmy Gatz, despite his ambitious self-reinvention, cannot have Daisy because he "isn't quite white enough" (Michaels 2006). Race thus serves as one of the foundation stones of what Fitzgerald—in other respects, perhaps not entirely credibly—seems to view as the lifelong immutability of birth status. At least a degree of racial subordination extends, moreover, not just to African Americans but also to the millions of people from immigrant families who were not, at the time, coded socially as being fully White unless (in Tom's term) they were "Nordic."

It's a Wonderful Life focuses entirely, and *The Wolf of Wall Street* predominantly, on White characters (although Jordan's band of merry men includes a "Depraved Chinaman"). So these works neither discuss race nor engage with how White supremacy might interact with issues of class. This comes as no surprise, and indeed is sociologically realistic, in a country as segregated as the United States—be it by neighborhood, profession, or family and personal ties.

Yet living just among Whites does not imply the subjective experience of living as if in an all-White country. Instead, it is clear in the broader culture that even Whites who never personally meet non-Whites are very conscious of living in a diverse society in which White supremacy has prevailed for centuries but is now subject to challenge.

Our violent racial history is so well known, and yet remains so fraught, that teaching it in the schools has become a hot-button cultural issue. Among this history's threatening implications is that Whites might someday face a reckoning. This fear—and perhaps an associated, even if suppressed, feeling of guilt—can give White identity a strangely beleaguered aspect.

Consider the classic scenario, from any number of Western movies (e.g., John Ford's *The Searchers*), in which isolated settlers on the frontier face the threat of a murderous "Indian" raid. This meme is readily adapted to modern urban settings, and to Black or Hispanic, rather than Native American, antagonists (e.g., *Fort Apache, The Bronx*). Likewise, consider urban vigilante films, like *Death Wish* and *Dirty Harry*, in which the violent White hero punishes non-White criminals, not just for their bad acts but for their insolence. A White hero's righteous violence may also be tied to defending White women. As we see in both *The Searchers* and Scorsese's *Taxi Driver* (in which a psychopath tries to act out the frontier hero trope in a seedy urban landscape), this impulse need not depend on the women's affirming that they want to be rescued.

In American history, White solidarity has frequently proved powerful enough to outweigh economic and class concerns. After the Civil War, poor Southern Whites allied with former slaveholders based on race, rather than with formerly enslaved persons based on class. In the 1960s, White backlash, reflecting unease about the pace of racial progress, realigned American politics to the right (Glickman 2020)—even without accompanying extreme high-end inequality or, until the end of the decade, economic stagnation. Trumpism offers a notorious modern replay, under more trying distributional and economic circumstances.

Trumpists' embrace, amid a pandemic, of a war against public health that cost many thousands of them their lives suggests that they do not view either politics or politicians through a conventional self-interest lens. Some have even expressed their willingness to "die for Trump" (Brewster 2020). This level of attachment, which goes beyond merely accepting him as an Ayn Rand superhero, suggests immense gratitude for his stance as Insulter-in-Chief, mocking both non-Whites and racially disloyal Whites. Questions of practical self-interest (and even physical survival) have evidently been outweighed by the causes of racial affiliation and point-scoring.

The anger that makes Trump's derision of Others so welcome reflects an affronted "desire for a type of conservative male dominance over all aspects of society, government, and culture, [that is] rooted in a specific strain of white evangelical arrogance" (Kurtz 2021). Yet this apparent arrogance does not entirely ring true. Like the rage of a Trump or a Galt, it bespeaks an underlying neediness and lack of secure self-respect. In this regard, our cultural tensions around market meritocracy and race may be dangerously intensifying each other.

Survey data show that Trump supporters generally do not come from among the nation's poor and often are decently successful in their business lives. Yet, given the broader media and online world that appear so unrelentingly on their (and our) screens, their attention keeps getting drawn to people whose success greatly exceeds their own. Under an American Dream credo, as ramped up by Randism, to the effect that such success is the supreme and indeed only measure of human worth, this may leave them feeling mediocre and small.

White supremacy offers potential palliation, by suggesting that at least one is superior to Them. But challenges to White supremacy then worsen the hurt. Millions of Trump supporters apparently feel hurt enough to embrace, not just conventional White backlash, but also a willingness to submerge their own egos and interests into the worship of a putative god-hero who makes no pretense of caring about anything or anyone except himself. A key psychic benefit, presumably, is that the god-hero's triumphs become their own, if only through fantasy identification.

While this is a familiar scenario in the history of cults, it has never previously been observed to this degree in American mass politics. It is not just a deadly danger to all Americans (including the Trump supporters themselves, given his pandemic-verified indifference to their welfare) but also a shocking diagnostic. Only in a grievously ailing culture could such a thing happen.

Over the last few decades, perhaps either America's fitful movement toward racial equality, or its economic travails—what with recessions and pandemics, the rise of the top 0.1 percent, and reduced upward mobility for the rest—would have been better tolerated had not the other been going on as well. But under this dual challenge, we may still be in the early stages of learning just how far negative American exceptionalism can go. And we may face a final crack-up, after centuries of mere tension, between the rival dictates of egalitarianism and democracy on the one hand and market meritocracy along with racism on the other.

*****

In the First Gilded Age, rising high-end inequality and its associated distempers eventually drew the political pushback of the Progressive Era. Then the malady itself substantially receded, due in part to the calamity of two world wars sandwiched around a decade-long Great Depression. Might its abatement—one would hope, through a less destructive mechanism than that of the years from 1914 through 1945—lie in our future once again? And might such an abatement even be accompanied this time—in sharp contrast to the Progressive Era—by substantial progress toward racial equality?

There is currently little ground for optimism. The calamity of the COVID-19 pandemic appears only to have increased high-end inequality, while also failing to convince Randites of the need for a cooperative social spirit. Meanwhile, assaults on democracy may degrade the political system's capacity to offer real or even symbolic pushback against the ever-increasing dominance of a remote economic elite. Perhaps only with a great deal of good luck—its provenance as yet undetectable—might our boats against the rising "maelstrom of recrimination, disrespect, and dysfunction" (Markovits 2019, x) finally be borne forward into a brighter future.

BIBLIOGRAPHY

Adams, James Truslow. 1931. *The Epic of America*. https://4.files.edl.io/96b7/08/27/19/
222028-c014eef6-9806-4b6f-a964-fe1b5524532b.pdf.

Agee, James. 1947. "Review of *It's a Wonderful Life.*" *The Nation*. February 15. https://
www.thenation.com/article/archive/its-wonderful-life/.

Basinger, Jeanine. 1986. *The It's a Wonderful Life Book*. New York: Alfred Knopf.

Berryman, John. 1946. "F. Scott Fitzgerald." *The Kenyon Review*, winter, Vol VIII, No. I.
https://kenyonreview.org/kr-online-issue/2013-summer/selections/john-berryman-
656342/.

Bewley, Maurice. 1954. "Scott Fitzgerald's Criticism of America." *The Sewanee Review*,
Vol. 62, No. 2 (April–June), pages 223–246.

Bicknell, John W. 1954. "The Waste Land of F. Scott Fitzgerald." 30 *Virginia Quarterly
Review*, No. 4 (Autumn), pages 556–572.

Bradley, Kit. 2016. "Criticism of John Galt's Speech in Atlas Shrugged – I Come Not to
Praise Johnny the G, But Bury Him." September 7. https://www.kitbradley.net/
posts/criticism-of-john-galts-speech-in-atlas-shrugged-i-come-not-to-praise-johnny-
the-g-but-bury-him/.

Bradshaw, Peter. 2014. "*The Wolf of Wall Street* – Review." *The Guardian*, January 16.
https://www.theguardian.com/film/2014/jan/16/wolf-of-wall-street-review.

Brewster, Jack. 2020. "Arizona GOP Asks If Republicans Are Ready to Die for Trump's
Voter Fraud Crusade." *Forbes*, December 8. https://www.forbes.com/sites/
jackbrewster/2020/12/08/arizona-gop-asks-if-republicans-are-ready-to-die-for-
trumps-voter-fraud-crusade/?sh=257dabf63edd.

Brody, Richard. 2013. "The Wild, Brilliant *Wolf of Wall Street.*" *The New Yorker*, December 24.
https://www.newyorker.com/culture/richard-brody/the-wild-brilliant-wolf-of-
wall-street.

Brody, Richard, 2014. "The Lasting Power of *The Wolf of Wall Street.*" *The New Yorker*, January 2.
https://www.newyorker.com/culture/richard-brody/the-lasting-power-of-the-wolf-
of-wall-street.

Brooks, David. 2021. "Our Pathetic Herd Immunity Failure." *The New York Times*, May 6.
https://www.nytimes.com/2021/05/06/opinion/herd-immunity-us.html.

Burgoyne, Robert. 2018. "Forms of time and the chronotope in the Wall Street film."
In Constantin Parvulescu, *Global Finance on Film: From Wall Street to Side Street*.
New York: Routledge, pages 42–55.

Burnham, Clint. 2016. *Frederick Jameson and The Wolf of Wall Street*. New York: Bloomsbury
Academic.

Canterbery, E. Ray. 1999. "Thorstein Veblen and *The Great Gatsby*." 33 *Journal of Economic Issues*, No. 2 (June), pages 297–304.

Capra, Frank. 1971. *The Name Above the Title*. New York: The Macmillan Company.

Carney, Ray. 1986. *American Vision: The Films of Frank Capra*. Hanover, NH: Wesleyan University Press.

Chalupa, Andrea. 2013. "F. Scott Fitzgerald on Writing *The Great Gatsby*." *Big Think*, May 9. https://bigthink.com/purpose-inc/f-scott-fitzgerald-on-writing-the-great-gatsby.

Cohen, Rick. 2010. "*It's a Wonderful Life*: The most terrifying movie ever." *Salon*, December 25. https://www.salon.com/2010/12/25/its_wonderful_life_terrifying_movie_ever/.

Corrigan, Lisa. 2014a. *And So We Read On: How The Great Gatsby Came to Be and Why It Endures*. New York: Little, Brown and Company.

Corrigan, Lisa. 2014b. "How *Gatsby* Went from a Moldering Flop to a Great American Novel." NPR interview, September 8. https://www.npr.org/2014/09/08/346346588/how-gatsby-went-from-a-moldering-flop-to-a-great-american-novel.

Cox, Stephen. 2003. *It's a Wonderful Life: A Memory Book*. Nashville, TN: Cumberland House.

Cox, Stephen. 2006. "On a Wing and a Prayer." *Los Angeles Times*, December 23. https://www.latimes.com/archives/la-xpm-2006-dec-23-et-wonderful23-story.html.

Cullen, Jim. 2003. *The American Dream: A Short History of an Idea*. Oxford, UK: Oxford University Press.

Decker, Jeffrey Louis. 1994. "Gatsby's Pristine Dream: The Diminishment of the Self-Made Man in the Tribal Twenties." 28 *Novel: A Forum on Fiction*, No. 1, pages 52–71.

Dimock, Wai-Chee. 2013. "Better Than the Yale Club." In *Los Angeles Review of Books*, "What's Left to Say? Four Fitzgerald Scholars on Baz Lurhmann's *Gatsby*." June 6. https://lareviewofbooks.org/article/whats-left-to-say-four-fitzgerald-scholars-on-baz-luhrmanns-gatsby/.

Donaldson, Scott. 2001. "Possessions in *The Great Gatsby*." 37 *The Southern Review*, pages 187–210.

Dreiser, Theodore, ed. 1931. *Hey, Rub-a-Dub-Dub! A Book of the Mystery and Wonder and Terror of Life*. London: Constable.

Duggan, Lisa. 2018. *Mean Girl: Ayn Rand and the Culture of Greed*. Oakland: University of California Press.

Eckart, Pablo, and Pablo Castrillo. 2018. "Financial Darwinism in Recent American Feature Films." In Constantin Parvulescu, *Global Finance on Film: From Wall Street to Side Street*. New York: Routledge, pages 56–67.

Edelstein, David. 2013. "Why I Sort of Liked *The Great Gatsby*." *Vulture*, May 7. https://www.vulture.com/2013/05/movie-review-the-great-gatsby.html.

Fitter, Chris. 1998. "From the Dream to the Womb: Visionary Impulse and Political Ambivalence in *The Great Gatsby*." Journal X, University of Mississippi, 3.1, autumn.

Flanagan, Thomas. 2000. "Fitzgerald's 'Radiant World.'" *New York Review of Books*, December 21.

Fraser, Keath. 1984. "Another Reading of *The Great Gatsby*." In Scott Donaldson, *Critical Essays on F. Scott Fitzgerald's The Great Gatsby*. Boston: GK Hall, pages 140–152.

Froehlich, Maggie Gordon. 2010. "Jordan Baker, Gender Dissent, and Homosexual Passing in *The Great Gatsby*." *The Space Between*, Volume VI:1.

Fryer, Sarah Beebe. 1984. "Beneath the Mask: The Plight of Daisy Buchanan." In Scott Donaldson, *Critical Essays on F. Scott Fitzgerald's The Great Gatsby*. Boston: GK Hall, pages 153–165.

Fussell, Edwin S. 1952. "Fitzgerald's Brave New World." 19 *ELH*, No. 4 (December), pages 291–306.

Gash, Chris. 2015. "How World War II Saved *The Great Gatsby* from Obscurity." *Mental Floss*, April 6. https://www.mentalfloss.com/article/62358/how-wwii-saved-great-gatsby-obscurity.

Gibson, Megan. 2011. "The Tea Party Movement and Atlas Shrugged." *The Guardian*, April 22. https://www.theguardian.com/commentisfree/cifamerica/2011/apr/22/tea-party-movement-republicans.

Glickman, Lawrence B. 2020. "How White Backlash Controls American Progress." *The Atlantic*, May 21. https://www.theatlantic.com/ideas/archive/2020/05/white-backlash-nothing-new/611914/.

Graetz, Michael. J. 2016. "'Death Tax' Politics." 57 *Boston College Law Review*, pages 801–814.

Haas, Elizabeth. 2015. *Projecting Politics: Political Messages in American Films* (2nd ed.). New York: Routledge.

Higham, John. 1959. "The Cult of the 'American Consensus': Homogenizing Our History." *Commentary*, February. https://www.commentarymagazine.com/articles/john-higham/the-cult-of-the-american-consensushomogenizing-our-history/.

Hilkey, Judy. 1997. *Character Is Capital: Success Manuals and Manhood in Gilded Age America*. Chapel Hill: University of North Carolina Press.

Jamieson, Wendell. 2008. "Wonderful? Sorry, George, It's a Pitiful, Dreadful Life." *The New York Times*, December 18.

Johnson, Robert. 2002. "Say It Ain't So, Jay: Fitzgerald's Use of Baseball in *The Great Gatsby*." 1 *The F. Scott Fitzgerald Review*, pages 30–44.

Johnston, Stephen. 2018. *Wonder and Cruelty: Ontological War in It's a Wonderful Life*. Lanham, MD: Lexington Books.

Kamiya, Gary. 2001. "All Hail Pottersville!" *Salon*, December 22. https://www.salon.com/2001/12/22/pottersville/.

Klein, Ezra. 2015. "Politicians Love the Middle Class. They Just Don't Know What It Is." *Vox*, January 27. https://www.vox.com/2015/1/27/7920749/what-is-middle-class.

Kracauer, Siegfried. 2012. *Siegfried Kracauer's American Writings: Essays on Film and Popular Culture*. London: University of California Press.

Krugman, Paul. 2009. "Making Banking Boring." *The New York Times*, April 9. https://www.nytimes.com/2009/04/10/opinion/10krugman.html.

Kurtz, David. 2022. "A View from Central Virginia." *Talking Points Memo*, November 4. https://talkingpointsmemo.com/edblog/trumpism-virginia-election-reaction.

Leary, Patrick. 2019. "What We Talk About When We Talk About the Middle Class." *The New Republic*, November 22. https://newrepublic.com/article/155702/political-meaning-middle-class-joe-biden.

Lucey, Bill. 2013. "Why It Took So Long for *The Great Gatsby* to Be Considered a Literary Classic." *NewspaperAlum*, May 13. https://www.newspaperalum.com/2013/05/why-it-took-so-long-for-the-great-gatsby-to-be-considered-a-literary-classic.html.

Maland, Charles J. 1980. *Frank Capra*. Boston: Twayne Publishers.

Markovits, Daniel. 2019. *The Meritocracy Trap: How America's Foundational Myth Feeds Inequality, Dismantles the Middle Class, and Devours the Elite*. New York: Penguin Press.

Marshall, Josh. 2014. "The Brittle Grip, Part 2." Talking Points Memo Editor's Blog. https://talkingpointsmemo.com/edblog/the-brittle-grip-part-2.

Martin, Brett. 2013. *Difficult Men: Behind the Scenes of a Creative Revolution: From The Sopranos and The Wire to Mad Men and Breaking Bad*. New York: Penguin Books.

McBride, Joseph. 1992. *Frank Capra: The Catastrophe of Success*. New York: Simon & Schuster.

Michaels, Walter Benn. 1995. *Our America: Nativism, Modernism, and Pluralism*. Durham, NC: Duke University Press.

Michaels, Walter Benn. 2006. "The Trouble with Diversity." *The American Prospect*, August 13. https://prospect.org/features/trouble-diversity/.

Murdock, Graham. 2018. "Narrating Finance Capital: Explorations in Speculation, Crisis, and Austerity." In Constantin Parvulescu, *Global Finance on Film: From Wall Street to Side Street*. New York: Routledge, pages 19–41.

Noah, Timothy. 2012. *The Great Divergence: America's Growing Inequality Crisis and What We Can Do About It*. New York: Bloomsbury Press.

Norton, Ben. 2015. "Libertarian superstar Ayn Rand Defended Native American Genocide: 'Racism Didn't Exist in This Country until the Liberals Brought It Up.'" *Salon*, October 14. https://www.salon.com/2015/10/14/libertarian_superstar_ayn_rand_defended_genocide_of_savage_native_americans/.

Ornstein, Robert. 1956. "Scott Fitzgerald's Fable of East and West." 18 *College English*, No. 3 (December), pages 139–143.

Orr, Christopher. 2013. "The Vulgar Genius of *The Wolf of Wall Street*." *The Atlantic*, December 25. https://www.theatlantic.com/entertainment/archive/2013/12/the-vulgar-genius-of-em-the-wolf-of-wall-street-em/282611/.

Pechter, William S. 1971. *Twenty-Four Times a Second: Films and Filmmakers*. New York: Harper & Row.

Pekarofski, Michael 2012. "The Passing of Jay Gatsby: Class and Anti-Semitism in Fitzgerald's 1920s America." 10(1) *The F. Scott Fitzgerald Review*, September. https://www.researchgate.net/publication/259551484_The_Passing_of_Jay_Gatsby_Class_and_Anti-Semitism_in_Fitzgerald's_1920s_America.

Person, Leland S. 1978. "'Herstory' and Daisy Buchanan." 50 *American Literature*, pages 250–257.

Philippon, Thomas, and Ariell Reshef. 2009. "Wages and Human Capital in the U.S. Financial Industry: 1909–2006." NBER Working Paper 14644, National Bureau of Economic Research. https://www.nber.org/papers/w14644.

Piketty, Thomas, and Emmanuel Saez. 2004. "Income Inequality in the United States, 1913–2002." https://eml.berkeley.edu/~saez/piketty-saezOUP04US.pdf.

Posnock, Ross. 1984. "'A New World, Material without Being Real': Fitzgerald's Critique of Capitalism in *The Great Gatsby*." In Scott Donaldson, *Critical Essays on F. Scott Fitzgerald's The Great Gatsby*. Boston: GK Hall, pages 201–213.

Rand, Ayn. 1963. "Racism." http://alexpeak.com/twr/racism/.

Rand, Ayn. 1974. "Address to the Graduating Class of the United States Military Academy at West Point, New York." http://fare.tunes.org/liberty/library/pwni.html.

Ray, Robert. 1985. *A Certain Tendency of the Hollywood Cinema 1930–1980*. Princeton, NJ: Princeton University Press.

Rollert, John Paul. 2014. "An Ethicist on *Wolf of Wall Street*: The Most Anti-Greed Movie Ever?" *The Atlantic*, February 26. https://www.theatlantic.com/entertainment/archive/2014/02/an-ethicist-on-em-wolf-of-wall-street-em-the-most-anti-greed-movie-ever/283806/.

Rosenbaum, Ron. 2012. "American Shylock: Arnold Rothstein (1882–1928)." *The New Republic*, October 24. https://newrepublic.com/article/109050/american-shylock-arnold-rothstein-18821928.

Rothman, Joshua. 2013. "The Serious Superficiality of *The Great Gatsby*." *The New Yorker*, May 13. https://www.newyorker.com/books/page-turner/the-serious-superficiality-of-the-great-gatsby.

Saez, Emmanuel, and Gabriel Zucman. 2014. "Wealth Inequality in the United States since 1913: Evidence from Capitalized Income Tax Data." NBER Working Paper 20625, National Bureau of Economic Research.

Savickas, Daniel. 2018. "Henry Potter Is the Undeniable Hero of 'It's a Wonderful Life.'" *Real Clear Markets blog*, December 14. https://www.realclearmarkets.com/articles/2018/12/14/the_message_of_its_a_wonderful_life_is_anti-prosperity_103539.html.

Scharnhorst, Gary. 1979. "Scribbling Upward: Fitzgerald's Debt of Honor to Horatio Alger, Jr." http://fitzgerald.narod.ru/critics-eng/scharnhorst-scribbing.html.

Schreier, Benjamin. 2007. "Desire's Second Act: 'Race' and *The Great Gatsby*'s Cynical Americanism." 53 *Twentieth Century Literature*, pages 153–181.

Schudson, Michael. 2004. "American Dreams." 16 *American Literary History*, pages 566–573.

Schulz, Kathryn. 2013. "Why I Despise *The Great Gatsby*." *Vulture*, May 3. https://www.vulture.com/2013/05/schulz-on-the-great-gatsby.html.

Scott, A. O. 2013a. "Shimmying Off the Literary Mantle." *The New York Times*, May 9. https://www.nytimes.com/2013/05/10/movies/the-great-gatsby-interpreted-by-baz-luhrmann.html.

Scott, A. O. 2013b. "When Greed Was Good (and Fun)." *The New York Times*, December 24. https://www.nytimes.com/2013/12/25/movies/dicaprio-stars-in-scorseses-the-wolf-of-wall-street.html.

Scrimgeour, Gary. 1966. "Against *The Great Gatsby*." 8 *Criticism*, No. 1 (winter), pages 75–86.

Serwer, Adam. 2018. "The Cruelty Is the Point." *The Atlantic*, October 3. https://www.theatlantic.com/ideas/archive/2018/10/the-cruelty-is-the-point/572104/.

Shackleton, Robert. 2008. "His Life and Achievements." In Russell Conwell, *The Acres of Diamonds Speech*. https://www.gutenberg.org/files/368/368-h/368-h.htm.

Shaviro, Daniel. 2020. *Literature and Inequality: Nine Perspectives from the Napoleonic Era Through the First Gilded Age*. New York: Anthem Press.

Sheffield, Rob. 2017. *Dreaming the Beatles: The Love Story of One Band and the Whole World*. New York: HarperCollins.

Silverman, Kaja. 1992. *Male Subjectivity at the Margins*. New York: Routledge.

Sirota, David. 2013. "Ayn Rand Is for Children." *Salon*, January 19. https://www.salon.com/2013/01/19/ayn_rand_is_for_children/.

Smith, Allan. 2021. "Birx Recalls 'Very Difficult' Call with Trump, Says Hundreds of Thousands of Covid Deaths Were Reventable." *NBC News*, March 28. https://www.nbcnews.com/politics/donald-trump/birx-recalls-very-difficult-call-trump-says-hundreds-thousands-covid-n1262283.

Snell, James. 2015. "When Historians Write About the Past, Are They Nearly Always Writing About the Present?" https://jamespetersnell.wordpress.com/2015/08/26/when-historians-write-about-the-past-are-they-nearly-always-writing-about-the-present/.

Spitznagel, Eric. 2013. "Q&A: Terence Winter on *The Wolf of Wall Street*'s Infamous Candle Scene." *Esquire*, December 23. https://www.esquire.com/entertainment/interviews/a26525/terence-winter-interview/.

Stallman, R. W. 1955. "Gatsby and the Hold in Time." 1 *Modern Fiction Studies*, No. 4 (November), pages 2–16.

Taylor, Aaron. 2007. "Twilight of the Idols: Performance, Melodramatic Villainy, and Sunset Boulevard." 59 *Journal of Film and Video*, pages 13–31.

Taylor, Derrick Bryson. 2020. "Alaska School District Votes Out 'Catch-22,' 'Gatsby' and Other Classics." *The New York Times*, April 29. https://www.nytimes.com/2020/04/29/books/palmer-alaska-school-board-books.html.

Taylor, Stephen J. 2015. "Go West, Young Man: The Mystery Behind the Famous Phrase." Hoosier State Chronicles: Indiana's Digital Newspaper Program, July 9. https://blog.newspapers.library.in.gov/go-west-young-man-the-mystery-behind-the-famous-phrase/.

Trilling, Lionel. 1945. "F. Scott Fitzgerald." *The Nation*, April 25. http://thenation.s3.amazonaws.com/pdf/1949.pdf.

Troy, William. 1945. "Scott Fitzgerald – The Authority of Failure." *Accent.* http://fitzgerald.narod.ru/critics-eng/troy-authority.html.

Veblen, Thorstein. 1899. *The Theory of the Leisure Class: An Economic Study of Institutions.* New York: The Macmillan Company.

Von Mises, Ludwig. 1958. "Letter to Ayn Rand." https://cdn.mises.org/Ludwig%20von%20Misess%20Letter%20to%20Rand%20on%20Atlas%20Shrugged_4.pdf.

Wade, Stuart. 2000. "Nick: What Went Wrong." *McSweeney's*, December 22. https://www.mcsweeneys.net/articles/nick-what-went-wrong.

Wall Street Journal. 2002. "Editorial: The Non-Taxpaying Class." November 20. https://www.wsj.com/articles/SB1037748678534174748.

Wasiolek, Edward. 1992. "The Sexual Drama of Nick and Gatsby." 19 *The International Fiction Review*, pages 14–22.

Wetts, Rachel, and Robb Willer. 2018. "Privilege on the Precipice: Perceived Racial Status Threats Lead White Americans to Oppose Welfare Programs." 97 *Social Forces*, pages 793–822.

Wheat, Alicia. 2013. "The Wolf of Wall Street." *People*, December 27. https://people.com/celebrity/see-thisskip-that-from- wolf-of-wall-street-to-walter-mitty/.

Wiencek, Henry. 2012. "The Dark Side of Thomas Jefferson." https://www.smithsonianmag.com/history/the-dark-side-of-thomas-jefferson-35976004/.

Wilkerson, Isabel. 2020. *Caste: The Origins of Our Discontents.* New York: Random House.

Willian, Michael. 2006. *It's a Wonderful Life: A Scene-by-Scene Guide to the Classic Film.* Chicago: Chicago Review Press.

Wilson, Edmund. 1941. "F. Scott Fitzgerald." http://fitzgerald.narod.ru/critics-eng/wilson-fsf.html.

Wolcott, James. 1986. "Less Than Wonderful." *Vanity Fair*, December. https://archive.vanityfair.com/article/1986/12/less-than-wonderful.

Wood, Robin. 2004. *Film Theory and Criticism: Introductory Readings* (6th ed.). New York: Oxford University Press.

Zinn, Howard. 2015. *A People's History of the United States.* New York: Bello.

INDEX